CW00541961

Praise for *Making Every History Lesson Count*

Making Every History Lesson Count is a great achievement and an important and very welcome piece of work. Illuminated by unfussy diagrams and charts, its six main principles are clear, sensible and disciplinarily authentic – and Chis Runeckles' writing is refreshingly free of confusing jargon, which helps make the book an accessible and pleasurable read. It draws on recent developments in cognitive psychology and is supported by the work of some of England's most original thinkers from both within and outside the history teaching community.

Trainee, newly qualified and less experienced teachers will find *Making Every History Lesson Count* invaluable, while department heads would be wise to read it too – as it has some powerful insights regarding the formation of sensible policy for the teaching of history. I wish I'd read it when I first started teaching.

Ben Newmark, Vice Principal, The Nuneaton Academy

History is a living subject and one that prepares children for the future by helping them analyse the past. In *Making Every History Lesson Count* Chris Runeckles draws out the subject's human aspect and communicates this with aplomb.

Chris' focus on research underpins long-standing "givens" around good teaching – knowledge, storytelling, questioning and the interrogation of resources – and invites teachers to enhance their own classroom practice and delivery.

A really useful guide for the busy history teacher.

Hywel Roberts, teacher, writer and humourist

Making every history lesson count

Six principles to support great history teaching

Chris Runeckles

Edited by Shaun Allison and Andy Tharby

Crown House Publishing Limited
www.crownhouse.co.uk

First published by

Crown House Publishing Limited
Crown Buildings, Bancyfelin, Carmarthen, Wales, SA33 5ND, UK
www.crownhouse.co.uk

and

Crown House Publishing Company LLC
PO Box 2223, Williston, VT 05495, USA
www.crownhousepublishing.com

First published 2018. Reprinted 2018.

British Library Cataloguing-in-Publication Data

A catalogue entry for this book is available from the British Library.

Print ISBN 978-178583336-6
Mobi ISBN 978-178583378-6
ePub ISBN 978-178583379-3
ePDF ISBN 978-178583380-9

LCCN 2018952173

Printed and bound in the UK by

TJ International, Padstow, Cornwall

Acknowledgements

While writing this book I have leaned heavily on my family, friends and colleagues; both in terms of allowing me the time and space to create it and for the ideas that it contains. Without them the process would have been impossible and I am indebted to them all.

This book is ultimately the manifestation of all that I have absorbed from the many professionals I have encountered throughout my career. I've been lucky to work in several great history departments, and there is something of all those colleagues I've taught alongside within these pages.

Of additional help have been the many colleagues I've encountered in other schools or across the varied world of social media. Everyone I've talked to or have asked to share their thinking has been gracious and generous, which has reminded me that we work in a genuinely supportive profession. Long may that continue.

Huge thanks must also go to Shaun Allison and Andy Tharby; first for giving me the chance to write this book and then for their insightful and thoughtful editing. I'm extremely lucky to work with you both.

The time during which I was writing coincided with my two daughters' first and third years respectively. Their smiles and love smoothed the process considerably, but it was the tireless work of my incredibly patient and brilliant wife that gave me the opportunity to write this book and is the defining reason why I've been able to do it. Thank you, Emilie, you're the best.

Finally, this book is dedicated to my mum. She is my greatest supporter and has forever been in my corner. Mum, I hope it makes you proud.

Contents

Introduction

When people are asked about their favourite, best or most memorable teacher at school, a disproportionate number seem to point to their history teachers. Perhaps this is just selective hearing on my part, but if really pushed I would say the phenomenon is real and must be down to something else.

For me, that memorable teacher was Mr Reddick, who taught A level history at the comprehensive school I attended in Dorset in the late 1990s. He only taught me one unit, British Politics, 1900–1939. Latterly, I've taught this topic myself, and have been a lone voice in support of its merits, fending off howls of derision from colleagues who would rather teach almost anything else. However, Mr Reddick's teaching had ensured that I would never lose my affection for this particular corner of history.

As my perpetual connection to this piece of history proves, our subject provides a unique opportunity to find moments of resonance with young people. When brought to life by a great teacher the past can captivate, amaze, infuriate and enlighten. It gives perspective to the lives we lead, and helps us make sense of the world around us by providing that most vital of contexts, the struggle of humanity through the ages. It can also be a source of solace in turbulent times to know that many of the troubles currently being played out on the world stage are in fact extensions or repetitions of previous events.

While Mr Reddick's passion was fundamental to his success as a teacher, alone it could not make his teaching brilliant. His successful practice was built on high expectation and challenge. He never dumbed down the detail or swerved the complicated political or economic machinations that are so vital to comprehending the politics of that time. Through captivating explanation he gave the era context and helped me place myself in the somewhat alien world of Westminster many decades previous. The feedback I received was thorough and precise and allowed me to hone my essay writing technique. Perhaps most importantly, he held the reins of discussion and debate through skilful and thought-provoking questioning. There were no gimmicks and nothing flash, just great teaching built on great knowledge of, and love for, the subject.

On returning to the classroom as a trainee history teacher seven years later, I found that the landscape had seemingly shifted. Independent learning was in vogue – and instead of refining the art of teaching, I was being trained to facilitate, with students expected to steer their own learning. Knowledge of the past seemed to be a commodity with little value, and we were taught that it was in fact the skills of learning that were important, with historical knowledge merely a conduit for the development of these. It felt wrong, and miles away from Mr Reddick's inspirational lessons.

Thankfully, in recent years much of this clutter has cleared away, with a welcome return to more traditional teaching approaches. In 2014 the Sutton Trust produced a report entitled *What Makes Great Teaching?*, which highlighted the following two factors as those linked with the strongest student outcomes:

- **Content knowledge.** Teachers with strong knowledge and understanding of their subject make a greater impact on students' learning.
- **Quality of instruction.** This includes effective questioning and use of assessment by teachers. Also shown to be important are practices including reviewing previous learning, scaffolding new learning and giving students adequate time to practise.[1]

---

1 Robert Coe, Cesare Aloisi, Steve Higgins and Lee Elliot Major, *What Makes Great Teaching? Review of the Underpinning Research* (London: Sutton Trust, 2014). Available at: https://www.suttontrust.com/wp-content/uploads/2014/10/What-Makes-Great-Teaching-REPORT.pdf, p. 2.

The importance of these factors will not necessarily be news to many teachers, but research of this kind does provide solid foundations to evidence the validity of the choices we make every day in our classrooms. A primary objective of this book is to synthesise the latest research on teaching and learning and make it specifically applicable to history teachers. There is a huge amount of evidence available, too much for a classroom teacher to be expected to engage with directly. This book does not claim to be an exhaustive review of educational research, indeed there will be areas not referred to as they fall outside of its remit. However, it does aim to bridge the gap between the world of academic research and the history classroom, which has been too big for too long.

Allied to an examination of research must always be the collective wisdom of history teachers who have, through trial and error, found out what works most often in their contexts. This book seeks to marry the evidence with collective experience; not only from my own classroom teaching but also from the expertise of my colleagues and from the insights of the many generous professionals who share their thoughts and experiences online. There are a variety of excellent teachers and thinkers who post blogs, write articles and engage with the debates surrounding history teaching via Twitter. I have referenced several, and would recommend their work as a further means of continuing professional development (CPD).

By pulling these strands together, this book seeks to explicitly articulate the fundamentals of great history teaching and provide practical strategies accessible to all classroom teachers. The framework for this is the six principles to support great teaching and learning shared by my editors and colleagues, Shaun Allison and Andy Tharby, in *Making Every*

Lesson Count: challenge, explanation, modelling, practice, feedback and questioning.[2]

These principles are not a lesson plan and do not form a neat hierarchy or have a prescribed order for use. They are to be interpreted by the individual teacher and should be thought of as the active ingredients for great history teaching. What they provide is a means to shape our practice and prioritise what is most important for successful classroom instruction. The principles are not strategies in themselves but, by making clear what we consider to be most important to high quality teaching, they allow us to narrow the focus and dispense with the unnecessary.

Each chapter explores a separate principle; with both a discussion on the underpinning theory and practical strategies for how the principle can be realised. There are points which contain a degree of idealism, as we all need to occasionally step outside the bubble of our day-to-day and allow our thoughts to turn to what might be possible. However, the book is rooted in pragmatism and aims to be useful to every history teacher, no matter their level of experience or context.

What the book is not is a silver bullet that can be fired into all contexts without interpretation. Each school, department, classroom and cohort is different, as is each teacher. There will be some for whom all of the suggested strategies and approaches will work and others for whom many may not. It is up to you to decide which you feel will be most useful and applicable. The subtle variations and additions you make will no doubt add richness to the original ideas and in many cases improve them.

The underpinning principle is *challenge*. This is the bedrock on which all the other principles are built and if pitched incorrectly no amount of skilful teaching can compensate.

2 Shaun Allison and Andy Tharby, *Making Every Lesson Count: Six Principles to Support Great Teaching and Learning* (Carmarthen: Crown House Publishing, 2015).

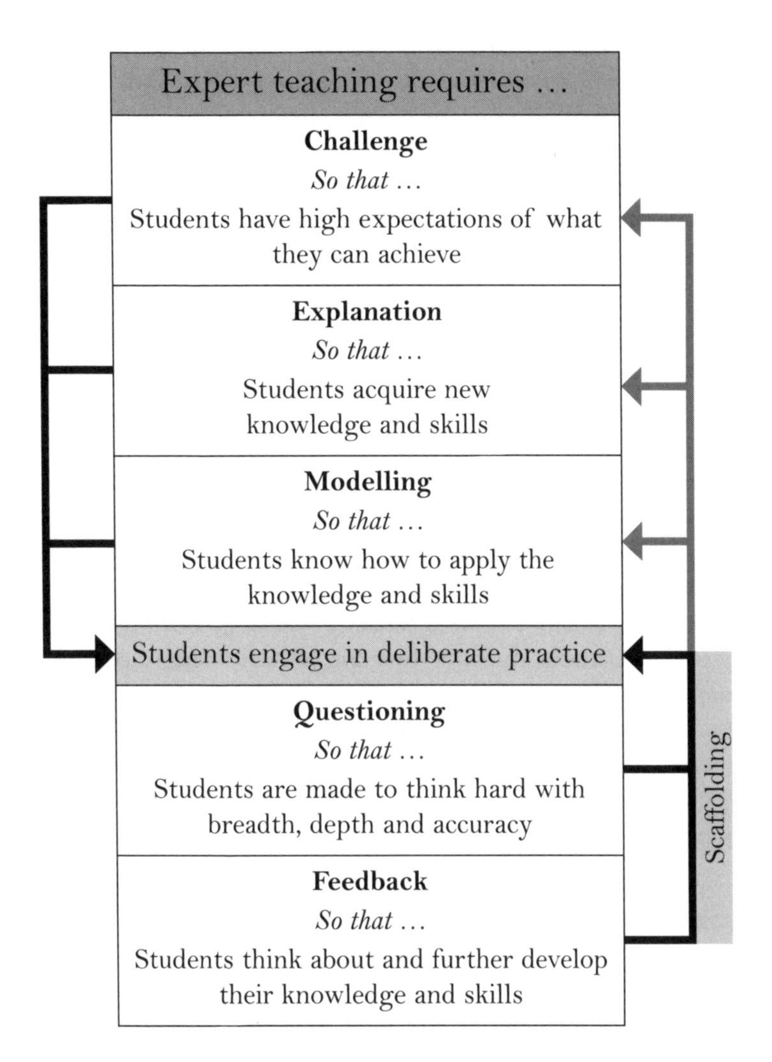
Expert teaching requires …
Challenge
So that …
Students have high expectations of what they can achieve
Explanation
So that …
Students acquire new knowledge and skills
Modelling
So that …
Students know how to apply the knowledge and skills
Students engage in deliberate practice
Questioning
So that …
Students are made to think hard with breadth, depth and accuracy
Feedback
So that …
Students think about and further develop their knowledge and skills
Scaffolding

We need to have the highest expectations of the level of challenge our students can cope with and not be afraid to embrace struggle as we help them pick their way through the more complicated pieces of the past.

Explanation and *questioning* are the most important tools that great history teachers possess. The storytelling and discussion elements of our discipline are vital in creating a representation of the past that young people can understand and interpret. The teacher's voice is unapologetically at the forefront of these strategies, with an emphasis on the importance of what we say to our students as well as how we say it.

Through the principles first of *modelling* and then of *practice* we will attempt to tackle how we can develop our students' fluency and competency with historical knowledge and extended writing. By modelling, we can teach our students primarily by using our own expertise, but also that of their peers, to demonstrate the knowledge, concepts and procedures vital to good historical thinking and writing. This strategy places the teacher, rather than pre-written structures, at the centre of this capacity building. With practice, we can support students to cope with the huge content demands of our subject, as well as with the complexity of our extended writing elements, all underpinned by the judicious application of *feedback*. The practical strategies included throughout this book ensure we can achieve these most challenging of objectives.

Running through each chapter are lessons from cognitive science about learning and memory. I firmly believe that knowledge of the events, people and places of the past should be at the front and centre of all history lessons. Historical knowledge is the most powerful legacy we can leave our students, as they will return to it every time they walk through the centre of a city or consider the decisions being made around them today. However, if we do not build our students' ability to retain the rich detail of the history that we deliver, then we will have failed to provide them with this gift, and what we have endeavoured to teach will drift and be forgotten. What we must continually strive to create are long-term, useable memories. Therefore, this book aims to demonstrate how cognitive science can be the history teacher's closest companion.

We are privileged to teach a subject that, whatever the changing tides of education bring, will always be one of vital importance. As British historian R. G. Collingwood said, "History is 'for' human self-knowledge … the only clue to what man can do is what man has done. The value of history, then, is that it teaches us what man has done and thus what man is."[3]

We may not be that memorable teacher for all our students, but we will be for some. The past is waiting to be taught.

Let's get started.

3 R. G. Collingwood, *The Idea of History*, rev edn (Oxford: Oxford University Press, 1994 [1946]), p. 10.

Chapter 1
Challenge

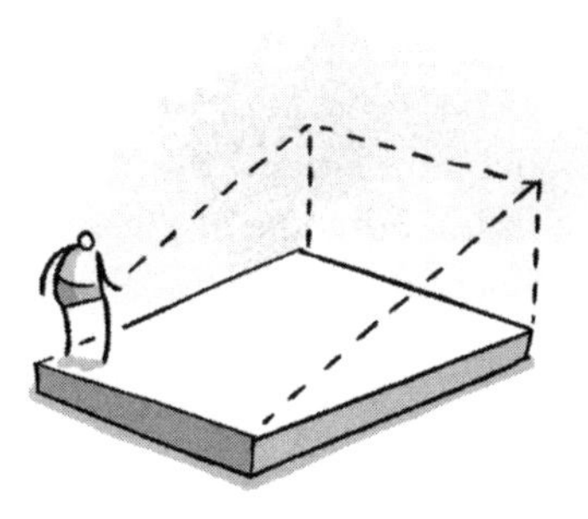

What to do about Evie

Evie is in Year 9 and does not like history. She cannot see the point in learning about people long dead or places she will never see. Outside of school she is not taken to monuments or museums, does not read for pleasure and does not engage in conversations that give the subject context. She daydreams her way through history lessons, completing the various tasks she is given to a standard that avoids drawing the teacher's attention, allowing her thoughts to drift away from the topic at hand. She does not find the majority of the work particularly difficult and is able to coast through lesson after lesson, with only occasional interruption from simple questions. When assessments come around she tends to struggle briefly before giving up. The subsequent targets she is set on how to better construct her answers make little sense as she doesn't understand the topic she is writing about. When it is time to complete her GCSE options form, history remains unticked.

We have all taught an Evie and it is all too easy to lower our expectations and allow her to be present in our lessons but rarely truly challenged. Frankly, in a lesson on the English Civil War, it is easier and requires less conflict to ask her to draw and label a picture of a member of Cromwell's New Model Army than to think about, and explain in writing, the reasons for Parliament's military success. The first may fill thirty minutes of a Friday period 5, while the second is going to take substantial time, effort and struggle. A caveat to this is that an adapted version of the first activity may contribute to a successful outcome in the second. Explaining the reasons for Parliament's success is an example of what might be termed critical thinking; however, we cannot think critically or deeply about history without the necessary subject, or domain, knowledge to think with.[1] Therefore, we must not fall into the trap of assuming that we should make our history lessons more challenging by moving more swiftly to critical thinking about the event, person or theme. We must first seek to develop our students' understanding, ensuring they have a secure base of knowledge about these topics.

In essence, history is a knowledge-based subject. We want our students to gain a deep knowledge and understanding of the past, and we should not confuse increasing challenge with neglecting the storytelling element of our discipline in order to jump straight into critical thinking or analysis. For students to be able to explain the New Model Army's success in the latter stages of the English Civil War, knowledge of the army's training and weaponry would be essential and time must be devoted to learning this detail. What is not essential is finding the right shade of brown to colour in a tunic, or selecting a particularly satisfying name for our freshly sketched soldier.

1 See Daniel T. Willingham, Critical Thinking, Why Is It So Hard to Teach?, *American Educator* (summer 2007): 8–19. Available at: https://www.aft.org/sites/default/files/periodicals/Crit_Thinking.pdf.

In the adapted version of Evie's task, she may spend a few minutes labelling a pre-drawn version of the soldier before adding her own line of explanation for each feature about how it would help him to be successful on the battlefield. Work done before, during and after this task would give her the context to make confident and well-informed observations and would define the success of this exercise. This can be achieved through the explanation, modelling and questioning strategies discussed in the later chapters of this book.

A transformational moment for me when clarifying what everyday challenge meant, was hearing Professor Robert Coe's keynote speech at the 2016 SSAT and The Prince's Teaching Institute conference. He posed three questions to the delegates:

---

1. *How many minutes does an average student on an average day spend really thinking hard?*
2. *Do you really want students to be "stuck" in your lessons?*
3. *If they knew the right answer but didn't know why, how many students would care?*[2]

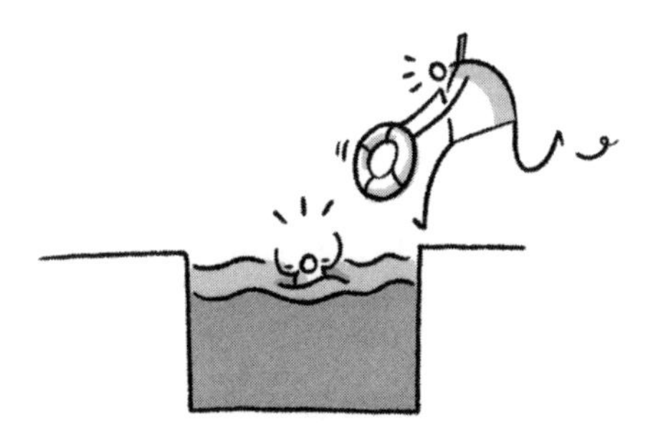

2 Robert Coe, What Makes Great Teaching?, speech at SSAT and The Prince's Teaching Institute Conference, 6 July 2016. Available at: https://webcontent.ssatuk.co.uk/wp-content/uploads/2016/07/08132401/What-makes-great-teaching-Rob-Coe-1.pdf, p. 12.

Question two particularly resonated with me. When I thought of my Evies, could I honestly say I regularly planned for them to be stuck? Or, more often than not, was I planning for them to be occupied? For the most part, the strategies in this chapter focus on how we can set our expectations high, up the challenge and, as a consequence, increase the amount of time our students spend thinking hard about history, struggling where necessary – while still keeping our sanity and an ordered classroom.

To add some underpinning theory to this, if we think about learning as happening in the three zones outlined in the model that follows, challenge is about getting our students into the struggle zone as regularly as possible. Learning is unlikely to happen in the comfort zone as they are not thinking hard enough about the material for it to be retained. Equally, once the challenge gets too high, students enter the panic zone and will shut down to what we are trying to teach them. This is in large part due to cognitive load theory, as when we offer students too much information their limited working memories will be overloaded. Cognitive science teaches us that our working memory only retains information for about thirty seconds before it is forgotten and that it can only cope with three to five different stimuli at a time. The information that we attend to and think about in our working memory will then transfer to our long-term memory, which is the storehouse of concepts, vocabulary and procedures. We ultimately want the content of our teaching to end up secure in long-term memory as it is from here that students can retrieve that knowledge.[3] Therefore, when the challenge becomes too high the working memory becomes overloaded and the knowledge is not retained.

3 John Sweller, Cognitive Load Theory, Learning Difficulty, and Instructional Design, *Learning and Instruction*, 4(4) (1994): 295–312. Available at: https://doi.org/10.1016/0959-4752(94)90003-5.

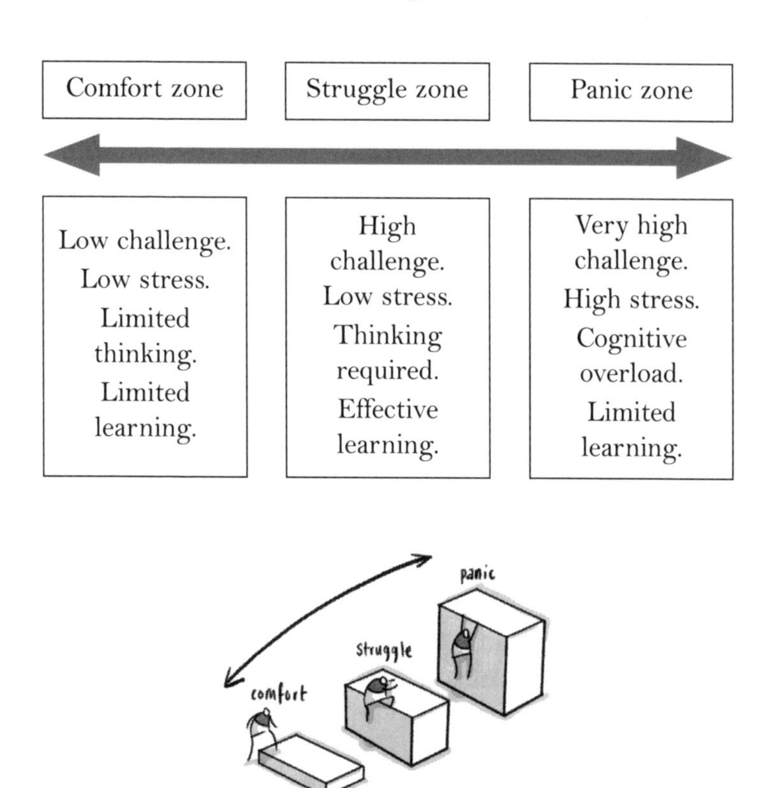

The lesson here is that it is important not to bombard students with sources of information, particularly if these compete for their attention. Therefore, if you are attempting to teach the Peasants' Revolt by explaining the events through storytelling, while also projecting a complicated slide on the board that contains a long piece of text to read, questions to answer and several images to analyse, students will have too much to cope with and will fail to retain the knowledge.[4] It would be better to complete your explanation and then unpick a key image, before introducing the text for them to read in silence and then, finally, ask students to complete the written outcome you desire, based upon the questions.

4 Sweller, Cognitive Load Theory.

Preparing for our students to get stuck and having the strategies to unstick them is a long-term venture and can best be encapsulated by the principle of challenge.

1. Prioritise Learning over Performance

Using plenaries at the end of lessons to prove to an observer that the students have made progress has always been a flawed measure. The reason why is that all they prove is surface learning, or performance, rather than deep learning. Learning is mysterious, liminal and invisible, and an individual lesson is the wrong unit of time over which to judge it.[5]

Recently I taught the Hungarian Uprising to a Year 10 class and the lesson went particularly well. I got the level of challenge right and the students dutifully struggled through the concepts and activities. At the end of the lesson I checked for understanding through questioning. All the questions I asked – from eliciting small factual details, such as the number of Hungarians killed, to checking more complicated concepts, such as the reasons for the USSR's military intervention – were correctly answered. It would be very easy at that point as history teachers to pat ourselves on the back and think, "Job done, they got that." However, the sad reality is that if I then failed to return to that topic regularly over the following weeks and months, faced with a question about it in the Year 11 mock exam, for the majority of those students all of that knowledge would have disappeared. They would not know who Imre Nagy was if he came into the exam hall and shook their hands, which is admittedly unlikely on several counts. Therefore the questioning at the end of the lesson revealed performance, not learning. It is learning we are seeking and so we should always think first about the macro rather than the micro; with regular

5 Nicholas C. Soderstrom and Robert A. Bjork, Learning Versus Performance, An Integrative Review, *Perspectives on Psychological Science*, 10(2) (2015): 176–199.

opportunities to revisit, revise and embed learning. In order for challenge to work it must be integrated into a stimulating curriculum that supports long-term retention of knowledge. Individual challenging lessons may be great in themselves but will not achieve our overarching aims.

2. Space It Out and Keep Coming Back

If the challenging curriculum we design is to work effectively we have to take into account the likelihood that students will forget what we teach them if we do not return to it regularly. As historians we tend to like chronology, timelines and stories. Everything in its proper place and taught in the correct order. However, this classic approach to the history curriculum may not be the most effective.

If we move through an epic topic like Germany, 1918–1939, constantly teaching new material, the reality is that however challenging we make the lessons, students will eventually forget what we've taught them if we never revisit the content. In the nineteenth century, psychologist Hermann Ebbinghaus conducted a series of experiments, the results of which revealed a trend which has latterly been termed the forgetting curve.[6] What he demonstrated was that we quickly forget newly learnt information unless we return to it repeatedly. Furthermore, the gaps in time we should leave before returning to that information can get increasingly larger after each revisit. So, after teaching the Munich Putsch for the first time you would ideally want to remind students of the key ideas within a day or so. Then you could leave it several days, then a week, two weeks, a month and so on until the information is fully embedded. The tricky part for history teachers is that we rarely see our students at such

6 Hermann Ebbinghaus (1913 [1885]), *Memory: A Contribution to Experimental Psychology*, Henry A. Ruger and Clara E. Bussenius (tr.). Available at: http://nwkpsych.rutgers.edu/~jose/courses/578_mem_learn/2012/readings/Ebbinghaus_1885.pdf.

regular intervals and so cannot quite manage this initial frequency. However, the principle still works even if you don't see them for a week at a time. You may just have to give more prompts to tease out the information.

This principle also fits with one of the strategies for learning with the strongest evidence behind it from cognitive science: distributed, or spaced, practice.[7] This is the idea that if you space out your study of a topic or concept over a length of time you will learn it more effectively than if you focus on it intensively for a short period. The implication of this for teaching history is for us to realise that studying the Munich Putsch in huge depth over two or three lessons but then not returning to it for several weeks would not be optimally effective, no matter how challenging and successful those initial lessons were. Therefore, we could devote less time to the topic the first time we teach it, but ensure we keep coming back to it, potentially adding extra layers of detail if necessary.

One method through which you can achieve spaced practice is homework. Rather than relating homework to what you are studying in class at the time, your homework tasks can be focused on topics previously studied. You can vary which topics tasks are focused on to help you keep a range of material alive with the students. Particularly if you feel time-pressured to cover a large chunk of content, this will help you find the balance between teaching the current topic and keeping the previous material going.

So a simple Key Stage 4 homework model could look like this:

7 John Dunlosky, Strengthening the Student Toolbox: Study Strategies to Boost Learning, *American Educator*, 37(3) (2013): 12–21. Available at: https://www.aft.org/sites/default/files/periodicals/dunlosky.pdf.

Main classroom teaching	Weekly homework schedule, repeat every four weeks
Topic 1	Topic 1, topic 1, topic 1, topic 1
Topic 2	Topic 2, topic 1, topic 1, topic 1
Topic 3	Topic 2, topic 1, topic 2, topic 1
Topic 4	Topic 3, topic 2, topic 1, topic 3

This does take substantial planning and forethought and ultimately needs all homework to be centrally planned within the department. Also, there is not an equal distribution of time spent on homework for all topics, so you will need to ensure your curriculum for topic 4 builds in strategies other than homework to embed knowledge (see the retrieval practice strategies in Chapter 4 for some ideas). However, this sequence follows the logic that those topics taught longest ago will require the most regular practice in order for the knowledge to remain accessible.

3. Set Single, Challenging Objectives

Once the curriculum has been organised in order to allow your challenging lessons to lead to long-term learning, you next need to think about breaking the learning down into smaller chunks. Traditionally we have thought of these chunks as hour-long lessons, indeed the title of this book implies that each lesson should be thought of individually. However, this is not to say that an objective cannot last beyond the confines of an hour, and it may be better to think more critically about how long each chunk of learning is likely to last. For example, the objective you give to your students might be:

Explain why the Liberals introduced social reforms in the early 1900s.

You may get this done within an hour, but if you feel ninety minutes would be the proper time needed to ensure you could explore the five generally accepted reasons in sufficient depth, then it makes sense to allocate this time, rather than be shackled to an arbitrary limit.

What is important is that we set single, challenging objectives. If we are to exemplify high expectations, any objective we share with our students should set the expectation for all. We certainly shouldn't limit some in our class to only being able to cope with certain aspects of the subject matter. To take our Liberal reform example, a "how not to" approach would look like this:

All students to identify why the Liberals introduced social reforms in the early 1900s.

Most students to describe why the Liberals introduced social reforms in the early 1900s.

Some students to explain why the Liberals introduced social reforms in the early 1900s.

Aside from the problem of assuming that explanation is inherently more challenging than description, this immediately sets most of the students in the room on the path to thinking that they are incapable of fully understanding the complexity of the topic about to be presented to them. We should set the objective as the "best case" outcome; what we really want our students to know, understand or be able to do. That is not to say all our students will find the same route to that objective or end up equally successful in meeting it. However, the starting point is high challenge for all.

4. Get Them Thinking Hard

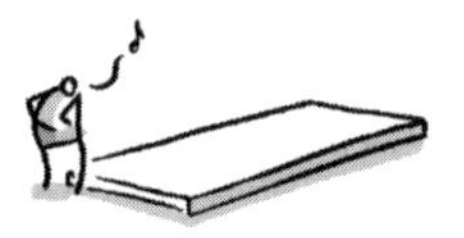

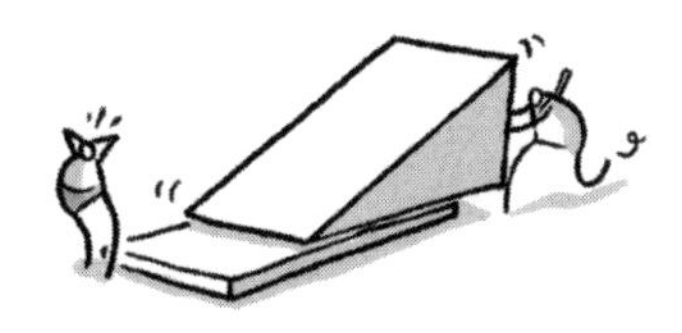

Returning to Professor Coe's three questions, we should plan to challenge our students as much through thought as through action, as his first question implies. Now, I'm not suggesting history teaching should become a purely cerebral pursuit in which we ignore students' exercise books and hold court in classrooms, conducting an undergraduate-style seminar. Extended writing and problem-solving activities will always be central to what we do. However, we should also plan for what we expect students to be thinking about throughout the lesson. As Daniel Willingham put it in his book *Why Don't Students Like School?*, "Memory is the residue of thought", therefore we need to get them thinking about the topic we are trying to communicate.[8]

We will only achieve this if we ourselves are thinking about when and how to deepen students' thinking. Ultimately, we

---

8 Daniel T. Willingham, *Why Don't Students Like School? A Cognitive Scientist Answers Questions About How the Mind Works and What It Means for the Classroom* (San Francisco, CA: Jossey-Bass, 2009), p. 54.

want to avoid the Evie scenario in which students skim across the surface of a topic without ever giving it careful consideration, because if they don't think about it they won't remember it. If your objective was to develop students' knowledge and understanding of the legal persecution of Jews in Germany during the 1930s, you may well use a timeline activity. Here, students may sort the jumbled cards detailing each law into chronological order and in doing so give little thought to the content, merely looking at the date. Some students may read and think about the laws, but this would be at random and not a necessary requirement for successfully completing the task.

However, you could add a layer to this activity that would be more conducive to careful thought. Turn the timeline into a living graph – so called because the content captured is continually debated and moved – with the *x* axis the time and the *y* axis a continuum from least to most serious in terms of consequence. Now students must make a judgement as they encounter each law, forcing them to read the detail carefully and think about the implications for the Jewish population. Students could still guess, and therefore bypass the thinking you are attempting to elicit, but you can head this off by structuring and sharing a follow-up activity. As students finish, have ready a written extension in which they have to justify why they have chosen a particular law as being most serious. You could then unpick the task through questioning, unearthing the thinking that has been happening.

5. Know Thy Historical Period

If we are to truly challenge our students then we need to have absolute confidence in our own knowledge base. Research demonstrates that a deficit in teacher subject knowledge can be a barrier to student achievement.[9] Unfortunately, one of the quirks of being a history teacher is that there will always be gaps in our knowledge; frankly we cannot know everything of significance that has happened in the past. This is something I've found myself explaining to teachers of other subjects on occasion. While there are Rosetta Stone principles that sit within history, an idea we will return to in Chapter 4 – such as the political spectrum, empires or economics – essentially, each period of history is distinct from another. Your knowledge of the American Revolution would certainly help you to understand the Indian independence movement in terms of the connections to the British Empire, but specific knowledge of the events, people and places would be totally unrelated. Therefore, if we are unexpectedly tasked with teaching a topic we haven't studied ourselves or taught before, it can be an intimidating prospect as we embark on our own journey of learning. As time goes on, the jigsaw that is human history gathers more and more pieces in our minds, and we build an increasingly comprehensive understanding, but we will always have our personal blind spots.

9 Coe et al., *What Makes Great Teaching?*, p. 2.

The default response can be to study the same textbook as the students and ensure you know that thoroughly. However, if your aim is to provide high and consistent challenge this will not be enough. As soon as you are asked a question that falls outside the parameters of the particular interpretation that the textbook or series of PowerPoints you've chosen gives, you will flounder. This floundering may then encourage you to narrow your teaching and retreat into student-led comprehension activities for fear that the gaps in your knowledge will be probed by curious students.

There are various ways in which to plug these gaps. One of my colleagues, George Eastment, always purchases the A level textbook corresponding to the new GCSE topic she is teaching. This is a manageable reading workload for her and allows that extra layer of knowledge for when students wish to probe a bit further. Obviously the ultimate solution is to read some "proper" history books. If nothing else they will give you an intellectual air as you sit by the pool on your summer holiday! The value of further reading was demonstrated to me recently, as a colleague of mine, Beth Clarke, was able to deepen my knowledge of Anglo-Saxon England. As a department, we were preparing to teach the rising against Earl Tostig in 1065. We all knew that one of the reasons for the uprising was high taxation, but because Beth had been reading widely she was able to tell us that, as part of the Danelaw region, Northumbrians paid just a sixth of the tax that the rest of the country did prior to Tostig becoming earl in 1055. This allowed us to explain to our classes with more weight why the rise in taxation was so hard to swallow for the people of the North. Ultimately, we need the confidence that sound subject knowledge gives us in order to push those we teach.

6. Use Challenging Vocabulary

A central tenet of teaching history should be that we use the rich language of the past, its people and its places. We should avoid at all costs the temptation to dumb down our language for fear that using the proper terminology will terrify our students. However, if we are to successfully create a classroom rich in historical language, we need to explicitly teach these words.

Vocabulary can be thought of in three tiers.[10] Tier 1 comprises words that are learnt through everyday common language use – for example, *book*, *cat*, and *smile*. Tier 2 words are those that are more prevalent in written language, contain multiple meanings and are important for reading comprehension – for example, *measure*, *fortunate* and *tend*. These words will often comprise the instructions within the questions we set students – for example, "explain why …" or "for an enquiry into …" Finally, tier 3 words are those that are tightly associated with a specific domain and usually only acquired as the need arises. So for history a word such as *wergild*, a system of fines in Anglo-Saxon England, would be tier 3.

There is some debate over what is more important for students. Marzano, for example, strongly advocates the explicit teaching of tier 3 vocabulary as a means of increasing students' background knowledge through secondary experience.[11] Conversely, Beck, McKeown and Kucan promote the explicit teaching of tier 2 vocabulary, claiming that these are words that students are likely to meet in different contexts, and so can help them to layer different dimensions of meaning and understanding onto a text or situation.[12]

10 Isabel L. Beck, Margaret G. McKeown and Linda Kucan, *Bringing Words to Life: Robust Vocabulary Instruction*, 2nd edn (New York: Guilford Press, 2013), p. 20.

11 Robert J. Marzano, *Building Background Knowledge for Academic Achievement: Research on What Works in Schools* (Alexandria, VA: Association for Supervision and Curriculum Development, 2004).

12 Beck, McKeown and Kucan, *Bringing Words to Life.*

The common-sense approach from a history-specific point of view is to teach both explicitly. Here are some ideas on how this could be done:

- **Knowledge organisers.** Create knowledge organisers (see Chapter 4 for a more developed explanation of what these are) that have both tier 2 and tier 3 vocabulary included. The first step to doing this is to debate within your departmental teams what that language is. It will vary substantially between topics and it will be time consuming the first time you try to unpick this.
- **Homework.** Develop homework tasks that test students' knowledge and understanding of tier 3 vocabulary. This should be based around retrieval practice rather than the initial learning of the words.
- **Sentence stems.** Students complete a sentence stem that contains the new word. For example, "In Anglo-Saxon England, the wergild was used to ..."
- **Test sentences.** Provide some sentences that make sense with the vocabulary and some that do not. For example, "The value of a wergild payment varied according to the person killed" or "The criminal was punished because he committed a wergild." Students are then asked to choose the correct sentence.
- **Visual images.** When introducing new vocabulary, ask students to draw a visual image that will help to explain what the word means. For example, depicting capitalism and communism using stick people.
- **Highlight it.** When giving back any assessed work or practice answers, ask students to highlight any tier 3 words, listed in their knowledge organisers, they used.

7. Set the Benchmark Early

It can be tempting to ease our students into a new term, year or key stage; to base our first lesson with a new class on some of the simplest and least taxing work they will do all year. The logic is that this eases them in and allows you to get to know them as you build up to something really challenging in a few weeks' time. The problem with this approach is that when students first arrive in your classroom they have no preconceptions, other than what friends or siblings may have passed on, about the expectations you will have of them. If you start off with some history bingo and a video clip they will breathe a collective sigh of relief and settle into their comfort zone. To then prise them out of this state will be tricky and require a lot of galvanising.

What is preferable is to use those first few lessons to set the bar of expectation high and handsome. Show them what you believe students in your class are capable of and get them to produce something similar. This is useful in a number of ways. It is something you can return to throughout the year, particularly in the dark days of early January, to demonstrate what they can do when they really put their minds to it. You also establish where the bar is in your classroom nice and early. We know students tend to meet the expectations we have of them, so start as you mean to go on. High expectations are not designed to scare them, so be careful not to come at it from a disciplinary stance. It is much more about instilling their beliefs of what they are capable of, and demonstrating your commitment to getting the absolute best out of them. Some practical tips for achieving this are:

- **Start with a worked example.** Use a particularly good piece of assessed writing from one of your previous year's classes. This will prove what can be done within the four walls they inhabit with you. Break it down and then get them writing something similar over the next few lessons.
- **Use a historical source with complex language.** Model with them how you can infer meaning from it and tackle the more difficult vocabulary together. Spend as much time as you need unpicking it before getting them to write some razor-sharp inferences.
- **Use a photo or political cartoon.** Choose one with a lot going on and get them to break each detail down until all possible messages and meanings have been extracted. The 1946 David Low cartoon reacting to Churchill's Iron Curtain speech would be a good one.
- **Get them thinking and making judgements.** Have a statement, such as "Blitz spirit was a myth", placed on a continuum ranging from strongly agree to strongly disagree and give students a series of sources that they need to place to indicate the extent to which they support the statement. This will require modelling by you to get them started.
- **Use historians' interpretations.** Find a couple of key interpretations about the topic you are about to study, and jointly unpick what you expect to learn about over the course of the topic based on what they say.

8. Share Excellence

Once examples of excellence have been created, make sure these are kept and shared. It is important that students understand the level of work you expect and that the level is achievable within the context of your classroom or department. The aim should be to immerse them in this excellence through displays and teaching strategies. Some practical ideas for how to do so are:

- **Create a portfolio of excellence.** The simplest way to do this is electronically. Scan or photograph the best examples and then file them according to year group, topic and question type. These can then be used as worked examples to provide a bank of benchmarks.
- **Focus your classroom displays on excellent historical writing.** Do not take up display space with particularly colourful or excitingly presented homework. Instead, find the very best pieces of extended writing and display those. Enlarge them if needed and draw attention to the very best parts with annotation. Use your displays to share what you will be most impressed to see in students' work rather than what might simply be aesthetically pleasing.
- **Share a great piece as you encounter it.** Either use the camera on your phone or a visualiser, if your classroom has one. As you circulate the class and encounter a great example of the task in progress, capture it, email it to yourself and project it onto the whiteboard to give some immediate whole-class feedback.
- **Showcase the best examples at parents' evenings.** Have some of the very best work done by the year group that term on display for parents and carers to peruse as they wait for their appointments.

Reflective Questions

- Do you plan for students to regularly get stuck and struggle in your lessons?
- Do you have high expectations of all the students you teach?
- Is your subject knowledge strong enough to stretch your students with confidence?
- How do you ensure students retain what you teach in their long-term memories and provide opportunities for them to retrieve this regularly?

Chapter 2
Explanation

Stuart's diligent frustration

Stuart is frustrated by his GCSE history lessons. He chose the subject last year, wooed by tales of courageous Spitfire pilots and deep injustice in the southern states of America. Stories like this from lessons in previous years, filtered through his teacher, have stayed with him. Since September, however, it feels like something has been lost – and instead of brilliant stories, Stuart is immersed in card sort activities and writing techniques. It is not that Stuart does not like or respect his new teacher; he always seems well prepared and organised, keeps the class busy and under control and has an excellent grasp on what students need in order to do well in the exam. The main difference Stuart has noticed this year is that his teacher rarely talks for very long and seldom tells the class directly about the people, places or events that they are learning about. As a result, Stuart often feels confused by the activities he is doing and untethered in the history the class is studying. Stuart dutifully arrives at his lessons and diligently completes the practice questions, redrafting tasks and homework, but often leaves with only a woolly understanding of what he's supposedly been learning. His book is beautifully ordered with countless activities completed, but when he comes to revise he finds it difficult to make sense of, or recall, the events that he wrote about. Stuart is starting to think he made a mistake in choosing history.

Many of the history teachers I know are prone to talking. However, in the not too distant past, many were shamed into curbing their instincts as "teacher talk" became a phrase to be feared. Observers timed, often literally, how long a teacher spoke to their class for, and recorded each passing minute as another black mark against their name. Thankfully the current has more recently been pulling us away from this sort of thinking, and we have started to venture back to the front and centre of our classrooms. The problem though, is the hangover. This can manifest in schools where the thinking has failed to shift. Only recently I was told of a colleague who was not progressed to the next stage of interview for committing the sin of too much talking. It also manifests in history teachers who, like me, were trained during the early 2000s and so were often taught to facilitate rather than instruct, with historical knowledge routinely placed below so-called learning skills in order of importance. Finally, the hangover effect is felt by teachers who feel they have lost the skill or confidence to explain well during the period in which the principle was neglected and underused.

This chapter therefore aims to reconnect us with what is perhaps *the* master skill of the history teacher: the ability as an orator to create within the students a sense of deep connection between themselves and the pieces of the past they discover through you. It is also to make the complex understandable, to help students to see the purpose of the lessons, to grasp the nature of what they need to do themselves, and to create memories that they can recall and use in the future.

As always, to be successful we must correctly interpret the concept, and while the strategies here focus primarily on what you say to your students, simply talking to them more is unlikely to significantly improve your practice. It is important to draw the distinction between talking and explanation, and to ensure that a desire to reconnect with one of the fundamental principles of great teaching does not lead to our students being talked at and confused.

There also comes a point in every lesson or teaching cycle when your voice cannot remain the sole conduit for transmitting new knowledge to your students. Learning in history requires layers of detail to be added to the frameworks that you set out, and some of this has to be achieved by students reading and processing information themselves. This forms a natural extension of our explanation and as such will form a small part of this chapter. However, these activities succeed or fail based on the explanation that precedes and follows them, and so it is our own explanation strategies that form the bulk of this chapter.

Every word we say should aim to make the task of understanding our subject easier, and as the expert in the room we are always – or at least should be – in the position where we know more about the topic we are teaching than our students do. As explained in Chapter 1, sound subject knowledge allows us to challenge our students. However, this can result in the "curse of the expert" effect, which is the counter-intuitive idea that being expert in something, while necessary, can bring its own unwanted baggage. In terms of evidence, the theory stems back to a doctoral psychology study done by Elizabeth Newton, which is unpublished but widely referenced in literature on the subject.[1] The study asserts that knowing something really well can make it more difficult to explain it to those who have less knowledge.

---

1 E. Newton, Overconfidence in the Communication of Intent: Heard and Unheard Melodies, unpublished doctoral dissertation (Stanford, CA: Stanford University, 1990).

Most history teachers would recognise the basic truth that our own familiarity with a topic, such as the causes of the First World War, can impede our ability to help Year 8 students understand it fully. We have made the connections many times before and so may forget to give a useful piece of context, such as the fall of the Ottoman Empire when teaching about the Balkans. For me, this concept should inform all of our explanations. We have previously, and repeatedly, connected the dots between cause and effect, change and continuity, significance and insignificance. Yet with each class we encounter we must find a way to break and then remake these connections as we teach them. This is undoubtedly difficult, with some evidence suggesting that the expert knowledge we possess will actually make it more difficult for us to explain it to novices;[2] hence the fact that simply being a brilliant historian will not give you the tools to teach history brilliantly. However, great subject knowledge

---

2 Nicole M. Hill and Walter Schneider, Brain Changes in the Development of Expertise: Neuroanatomical and Neurophysiological Evidence about Skill-Based Adaptations. In K. Anders Ericsson, Neil Charness, Robert R. Hoffman and Paul J. Feltovich (eds), *The Cambridge Handbook of Expertise and Expert Performance* (Cambridge: Cambridge University Press, 2006), pp. 653–682.

is undoubtedly essential and is the foundation stone for all teachers, as when its breadth and depth increases, so does the teacher's ability to explain, model, question and provide useful feedback. So, knowledge is, on balance, more of a blessing than a curse. Therefore, what we need, and what this chapter aims to provide, is evidence-informed explanation techniques that can overcome this natural barrier.

If you have read the book that began this series, *Making Every Lesson Count*, you will know that many of the strategies for great explanation have been inspired by Chip and Dan Heath's *Made to Stick*.[3] It lists six "sticky" principles, reinforced by the mnemonic SUCCES: simple, unexpected, concrete, credible, emotional and stories, aimed at making ideas stick by creating a lasting impression on the memory. All these principles are relevant and accessible to history teachers, but some more readily than others. Stories are essentially what we deal in – ours just happen to be real – and most, if not all, of our topics provide ample opportunities for emotional resonance and are rich in the unexpected. The other three take a bit more thought. Simple, in our context, means to strip out the unnecessary and focus on the core concepts while tethering what you teach to something that the students already know. History teachers are notoriously rubbish at cutting content – the curse strikes again – and it can be difficult to find that connection to a 12-year-old's prior knowledge when you're teaching them about the vagaries of the Stuart parliament. Concrete and credible also throw up some problems as the past is often an alien world, and providing opportunities to make it seem real, meaningful and ultimately believable can be hard. Hard but not impossible, though, and several of the strategies in this chapter are designed to bridge the gap between the worlds of the past and of our students.

In order to both make our teaching stick and escape the trap Stuart's teacher has fallen into, we need to embrace

3 Chip Heath and Dan Heath, *Made to Stick: Why Some Ideas Take Hold and Others Come Unstuck* (London: Arrow Books, 2008).

explanation. This can be a liberating change to your teaching, as anchoring your lessons in what you say to your students – rather than what you expect them to do – often feels more natural. The best explanations will be punctuated with questioning and transition regularly into modelling, practice and feedback, but explanation remains the foundation for these other principles. Ultimately, we should no longer be afraid to tell students what we want them to know or do.

1. Tell the Story

A former colleague of mine, Rob Sweeney, used to say to me that when he taught the Battle of Britain he ignored the first part of the lesson on the scheme of work and would instead tell his Year 9 class the story of the conflict. The prescribed activity involved students answering some comprehension questions about the context of the battle, before moving on to a card sort in which they categorised the reasons for

Britain's success. Rob's rationale was, why waste the opportunity to tell them a great story that he knew from years of practice would captivate his classes and, importantly, make everything he did with the students from that point on much easier and more successful? His approach was based on experience, but is supported by evidence. Psychologists have found that stories are "psychologically privileged" and that we have a greater ability to remember information when presented as narrative.[4] Unlike in other subjects, we don't have to search for the story within the content, we just need to ensure we don't lose them among all the other teaching clutter.

The tension here, though, is that when we encounter students' extended writing that reads like a story, we will generally criticise it in our feedback by saying that it lacks explanation, links or judgement. This is because we know that the best historical discourse contains more than just a description of events. However, to stay true to the story as we are telling it, we can't constantly be adding the analysis as it would become too confusing.

The history department at Huntington School in York have got around this problem by using macro stories, starting each unit with a one-lesson narrative overview of the whole topic.[5] Essentially, they summarise all the content into a story that can be told in an hour. In doing so, they give their students a map of the basic landscape of the period of history they plan to inhabit in the forthcoming lessons. From there, they can add layers of analysis and inference to build the picture in a manner that allows students to see not just the narrative but also the detail and important links, such as cause and consequence. In this way, the teaching is rooted in the story but also recognises that our role as history teachers does not start and finish with the narrative.

---

4 Willingham, *Why Don't Students Like School?*, p. 66.

5 Hugh Richards, Telling Stories and Teaching History, *Research Schools Network* [blog] (5 June 2017). Available at: https://huntington.researchschool.org.uk/2017/06/05/telling-stories-and-teaching-history/.

2. Plan Your Storytelling

Despite having been sent scores of lesson plans by teachers I have been due to observe, I can't remember reading a single one that said, "Tell them the story of …" Perhaps this is unsurprising given the climate around teacher talk mentioned previously; however, for our stories to hit home reliably, we need to plan them. The starting point here is subject knowledge; if you know the period inside out, you will know which sections will best lend themselves to being delivered in this way. For example, the start of a rough lesson plan with the objective of students learning the events of the Cuban missile crisis might look something like this:

---

1. *Open curiosity gap by displaying photos taken by U-2 spy planes. Description task.*
2. *Tell story of how the photos were brought to JFK in his bedroom on 16 October 1962, of how ExComm subsequently met, and of the options they debated. Refer to hawks and doves split.*
3. *Consequences activity based on ExComm options.*

If your knowledge of the Thirteen Days is not fully secure – and, let's face it, the fine detail of fiddly topics like this are easy to get wrong if you haven't done a bit of knowledge recall of your own recently – then you may be tempted to veer away from telling the story yourself and retreat into the security of a PowerPoint presentation, textbook, worksheet or card sort activity. However, none of these approaches would have the power of you telling the story yourself, complete with your own anecdotes, asides and interactions. Therefore, when preparing for a lesson or series of lessons, first identify the sections that you feel would work best coming from you: something that will be very topic-specific. Then make sure you know those sections well enough to deliver them as confidently and accurately as you would relay a story to your friend about a minor celebrity you bumped into in town the previous evening. The planning time you devote to this may not produce a satisfying resource but it will ultimately be just as useful.

3. Emotive Explanation

The idea that students need to be sat open-mouthed in a state of joyous captivation in order to learn has been pretty widely dismissed, with evidence stacking up that enjoyment and a positive attitude are not the keystone to learning.[6] However, they do need to be paying attention. Students remember what they think about so we need to make sure their focus is on the story we are telling and not on the particularly offensive colour combination we chose to pair in today's outfit, or on wondering why the display behind us still contains work from three years ago. If we don't, sadly, this is what they will remember. Therefore, we need to get them paying attention and make what we say something that they will think about. Emotive explanation can help us here, particularly as, as already mentioned, emotion is proven to aid retention by helping ideas to stick in our memories.

The story of William the Conqueror's harrying of the North could be told with or without the addition of emotion. You could simply describe it as a method of control through which William helped his transition from invading foreigner to established monarch, focusing on the big picture implications and historical significances. Useful stuff. Or you could use tone and language to pull on the emotional heartstrings a bit. I find the big-to-small approach can be a useful

---

6 Stephen Gorard, Beng Huat See and Peter Davies, *The Impact of Attitudes and Aspirations on Educational Attainment and Participation* (York: The Joseph Rowntree Foundation, 2012), p. 45. Available at: http://www.jrf.org.uk/sites/files/jrf/education-young-people-parents-full.pdf.

strategy here; going from the macro to the micro, with the implications thrown in at the end. For example:

He burnt down the farms (pause), *he murdered the people* (pause), *he slaughtered the livestock* (pause), *he smashed all the tools* (pause); *in fact, he even destroyed the carefully stored seeds and ground salt into the soil* (pause). *In doing so, he laid waste to the area not just for the short-term but for a generation.*

Your body language will also be important here. Gesture, eye contact and facial expression all play their part. If this is not something that comes easily, speak to the drama department – who are generally excellent at this – about observing their best teacher.

This is not to say we all have to become that overly enthusiastic and rather annoying guide from the last Year 9 trip to a historical monument. We are teachers, not entertainers. However, we should not ignore the power and value of using emotion to stimulate deep thought and create memories.

4. Create a Sense of Mystery

Another lesson from the Heath brothers is the idea that if we open up a curiosity gap, alluded to in the lesson outline in Strategy 2, students will naturally want to fill it, thereby stimulating their thinking.[7] Rather than revealing the whole story immediately we can tease students with snippets and snapshots to create intrigue and suspense. This can be done very effectively using images. The iconic photo of Kim Phuc running naked from the napalm attack on her village, flanked by US soldiers, drops students straight into the heart of the Vietnam War. From this photo, questions can be generated to develop curiosity. For this particular example you could ask students to generate five questions they have about the picture, with the condition that each must start with a different question word: who, what, when, where and why. You could then ask students to return to these questions at the end of the lesson to see which they can answer. Any they cannot could then direct your final discussion.

Another technique is to use enquiry questions. For example, start your unit on the English Civil War by posing the question, "Why was the King of England publicly executed in 1649?" The aim is that students will want to solve the puzzle and will therefore be more inclined to work through the problems to get them there.

5. Anecdotes and Asides

The more we teach and the more we read the more we add to our ability to embellish. These optional extras can often be the *unexpected* to go with the emotional. Remarking on Soviet leader Leonid's fondness for greeting foreign dignitaries with enthusiastic kissing – as revealed by any video of every major summit meeting he was involved in – when teaching the Brezhnev Doctrine, or on Elizabeth I's rotten teeth when teaching the Tudors, or on the tidal wave of sewage that flowed through London when teaching the Industrial Revolution would all be good examples. These

7 Heath and Heath, *Made to Stick*, p. 84.

nuggets can be used to provide a spike of the unusual or surprising to our explanations that can help solidify those much sought-after memories. The trick here is to first develop sound subject knowledge. Many historical anecdotes are in fact fiction, as we will all have found when trying to weed out misconceptions about Hitler from a Year 9 class. We need to know the difference and ensure that we do not relay false, if entertaining, asides.

Finally, a word of caution that without careful handling the anecdote can supersede the core knowledge. Most teachers will have experienced the exasperation of a class remembering a fairly useless bit of colour when they cannot recall the significant details that underpin the concept. However, with judicious use, anecdotes and asides can be the hook that draws students into the knowledge you need to transmit.

6. Analogies

Much of the past is an alien world to your average 14-year-old, and one of the most successful ways of helping them to navigate it is to use analogies to explain what can often be quite abstract concepts. Research supports this approach, as is well-illustrated by the concept of concrete examples, one of Megan Smith and Yana Weinstein's – the Learning Scientists – six strategies for effective learning.[8] While not exclusively focused on analogies, the concept – using specific examples to comprehend abstract ideas – is transferable.

A classic example of this would be when explaining how the alliance system led to the start of the First World War. Your explanation could look something like this:

---

8 Megan Smith and Yana Weinstein, Six Strategies for Effective Learning, *The Learning Scientists* [blog] (18 August 2016). Available at: http://www.learningscientists.org/blog/2016/8/18-1.

It is very much like a falling out at lunchtime. Two people start an argument and then begin to worry that the other person might be getting their friends involved. So what happens is that both individuals gather a bigger and bigger group of people who agree to join in. Before long, what started out as a disagreement between two people becomes a much bigger problem.

The best analogies can be used as an anchoring point and returned to throughout the topic. An opportunity to extend the previous example would come when you reach the Treaty of Versailles:

If you remember the lunchtime argument, it would be like taking the person who lost and saying they were the one who started it, just because they happened to lose. They would be the only one the teachers punished, have to apologise to everyone else involved and have to do the victor's homework for the rest of the year.

In my experience, the outrage caused by this example far exceeds that expressed when looking at Article 231, the war guilt clause, in its own terms.

The reason why school-based examples are particularly useful is because the most effective analogies need to be rooted in something that all, or nearly all, are very familiar with. Sports analogies are often tempting – and can work well – but be careful, as you can easily confuse students further if you contrive to explain an abstract idea through something they are equally unfamiliar with. For example, you might compare the stalemate of the Western Front to a dour Premier League 0-0 draw from the previous weekend. However, for those in the class with no footballing knowledge or interest, the comparison will mean little. We are trying to find that illustrative example that helps our students make sense of the more difficult and unusual events of the past.[9]

Analogies can also be used to help explain abstract ideas connected to particular procedures you wish the students to complete, as opposed to specific pieces of historical knowledge. A good example of this would be when you first attempt to explain how to judge the relative usefulness of sources. I struggled with this for years and my explanations often ended up confusing students and ultimately led to poor answers. I now use the following analogy:

It's as if there were an historian locked away in a hut high up on top of a mountain. This historian has never heard of the topic we are studying and has no access to any information other than the particular source we are looking at. To work out the usefulness of the source, first think about what our historian could learn from it, but also what information would be missing and how this might mislead.

What this does is temporarily isolate the source from any other contextual knowledge that the students may possess. In doing so, it allows you to communicate the seemingly abstract principle of source usefulness in a concrete and tangible way.

As with all explanation techniques, analogies will work best if you plan them. It is easy to head down the cul-de-sac of an imperfect analogy, only to find yourself reversing quickly out again.

9 Katherine A. Rawson, Ruthann C. Thomas and Larry L. Jacoby, The Power of Examples: Illustrative Examples Enhance Conceptual Learning of Declarative Concepts, *Educational Psychology Review*, 27(3) (2015): 483–504. Available at: https://doi.org/10.1007/s10648-014-9273-3.

7. Lift the Veil

One potential effect of the curse of the expert is that we expect students to automatically recognise the value in what we ask them to do. We know that creating a timeline of all the changes to punishment in the early modern period will help students make sense of, and consolidate, the varied and contrasting events we've been studying for the past three weeks, but we often forget to share that wisdom with them. Since getting on board with the six principles for great teaching and learning, this is almost certainly the most common target I've given post-lesson observation: *tell* the students the *purpose* of the task you are asking them to complete. Our plans – short-, medium- and long-term – for where we want go with our students, and what we intend them to learn, should be explicitly shared. In reference to the timeline example, the explanation could look like this:

> *We've covered an awful lot in the past four lessons about changes to punishment in the early modern period, so for the next twenty minutes or so we are going to draw that together using a timeline. This will help us to organise those changes into a chronology* (opportunity to question about the meaning of the term chronology) *which will show us how they fit with everything else that was happening at the time and how all these components relate to each other. Also, it will be a good way to remind ourselves of the detail and a great way to get those memories to stick. Every now and again it is really important to pause like this and go over what we've been learning recently to stop the knowledge being forgotten and to ensure we can see how it all fits together. So, what I want you to do is …*

In my experience, teachers often start with the "So, what I want you to do is …" before explaining to students why that is. An essential function of great explanation is to lift the veil on what we are thinking and why we are asking students to do something. The evidence from the Education Endowment Foundation (EEF) Teaching and Learning Toolkit around metacognition suggests that getting students to think about their learning more explicitly has a fairly dramatic positive effect.[10] Metacognition is a rather slippery concept and connects to some degree with all learning. To simplify it slightly, metacognitive strategies aim to improve how well students are able to plan, monitor and evaluate their learning and develop the tools they need in order to do so effectively. We will return to this at various points throughout the remaining chapters.

One element of developing metacognition involves giving students an insight into why they are doing what they are doing at any given moment in a lesson, and equally in a series of lessons, a half-term or a year. This will allow them to see how the current work fits into their wider learning and then to monitor and evaluate it. If done successfully you will notice that the lull which seems to occur when you have finished explaining what to do, but inexplicably only about a third of the class seem to be doing anything, will start to disappear. Once they get the purpose as well as the instructions, most students will engage with the task. This will also limit the number of individual questions you get from students who have failed to tune in to the short, activity-focused instructions and so need their own private lesson on what to do. This is very much a "we're in this together" technique, with you as the teacher involving them in the whole process of learning, including the thinking behind it, rather than expecting them to blindly follow your instructions. We wouldn't get on a train without knowing where it was going – except perhaps after a particularly bad Year 9 class – so we shouldn't expect our students to do the equivalent in our lessons. It may seem obvious, but completing a quick mental check when you notice that students are struggling with

10 See https://educationendowmentfoundation.org.uk/resources/teaching-learning-toolkit/meta-cognition-and-self-regulation/.

something, by asking yourself whether they would be able to tell you the way in which what they are doing will be of use to them, is a good habit to get into. This is a cultural thing and needs to be built up over time, but it will help them become more self-regulating and therefore more in tune with your objectives, and hopefully less like confused passengers.

8. Add the Extra Layers

We always have a huge amount of content to communicate and not all of it can simply be explained by the teacher. As mentioned previously, the starting point for a topic should always be your explanation. However, this will not be sufficient to cover all the fine detail, as in order to do that we would never stop talking. Revealing the layers of history will add an indispensable richness to students' understanding of the past. Often it is the small details, such as the precise chronology of the events of 1793, which make a complex topic like the French Revolution make sense. Therefore, history teachers will always need a bank of strategies to hand to provide the necessary extension to our own explanation.

The potential pitfall with this approach is that our teaching becomes activity-led rather than objective-led. We can focus too much on what the students will be doing and not enough on what they will be thinking about and, by extension, learning. This can be a barrier to effective teaching and result in students drowning in complex worksheets filled with intricate and hard-to-explain tasks. In the worst instances, students will learn more about how to complete a particular type of activity than they will about the history they are studying.

Therefore, when choosing which activities to use for this phase of learning, always consider first how each will help students meet the objective you have set. Struggle and hard thinking are desirable, but only if they are targeted towards increasing students' knowledge and understanding of the past, and not on how to fill in a particularly fiendish table. A simple check would be to think through how you would approach the task yourself, and to consider how much cognitive work you would be devoting to the knowledge and how much either to deciding how to tackle the task or to the physical process of completing it – for example, how to arrange your card sort or how to present your work. Also consider the format that the students' notes will take. You will need to explicitly model the process involved in each new task and the output you are expecting students to produce, be that a mind map, table, bullet-pointed notes or written answers to comprehension questions.

An almost inexhaustible supply of resources has been created over the years and history teachers are extremely generous in sharing them online if you are looking for inspiration. You will naturally find the ones that you are most comfortable with and they will become your go-to options. Below are a few examples that work in most situations:

- **Textbooks.** These are unduly maligned in my opinion and, if carefully chosen, are still a must-have for the history classroom.
- **Knowledge organisers.** A one-page collection of the key knowledge, vocabulary and concepts for a particular topic.
- **Card sorts.** I'm not against card sorts per se, but think that we need to be wary about their use and application, keeping in mind the basic idea that students must be forced to think about the content, rather than just organise it according to chronology. Try to avoid cutting and sticking and instead number the boxes in order to manipulate the information.

- **Information sheets.** Declutter these are far as possible so that, together with a few key images, only the most vital information is included.
- **Timelines.** A simple chronology is an excellent starting point for understanding any historical period.
- **Matching tasks.** These work well for linking cause and consequence.
- **Packs of historical sources.** Can be categorised, used for comprehension activities or to provide evidence on either side of a historical debate.

9. Find Someone Who Explains It Better

Sometimes despite all our skills as orators we have to admit defeat, stand back and let someone else – who, frankly, will do it better – explain something. Modern classrooms are blessed with a portal through which we can bring a variety of historical figures, first-hand witnesses or expert historians into the room. My former colleague, Jack Tyler, developed and shared some innovative strategies for using video clips in the history classroom as a useful addition to the voice of the teacher.[11] One of his ideas was to aid the teaching of historical interpretation by using clips of Hollywood trailers that over-inflate the role of particular individuals, such as William Wilberforce's contribution to abolishing the slave trade as propounded by the 2006 film *Amazing Grace*.

Another was to use video clips to bring a topic to life. For me this works best with modern history. My personal favourite is to use some of the many testimonies gathered by the United States Holocaust Memorial Museum when teaching Kristallnacht. These wonderfully put-together clips of elderly people talking with dignity and composure about how the Nazis, and even their own neighbours, rifled through their possessions, beat their parents or burnt their synagogues give power to the event in a way that my second-hand interpretation simply cannot. Equally, why not hear Stokely Carmichael explain in his own words his anger and frustration with the injustices faced by black Americans during the 1960s, or Eugene "Bull" Connor offer his unique perspective on the merits of segregation. We have these, and an endless archive of similar clips, at our fingertips for when we feel our own version of events may fall short of the original experience.

There are, however, a number of caveats to remember when using video. The clips must be used judiciously and should be relatively short. Having a few comprehension questions to go with them will help students to filter and recognise the most significant points and retain the messages in the long-term. Clips should also be bookended by your own explanation – first setting the context and then, with the aid of questioning, exploring interpretations.

11 Shaun Allison, Effective Use of Video in the Classroom, *Class Teaching* [blog] (23 January 2014). Available at: https://classteaching.wordpress.com/2014/01/23/effective-use-of-video-in-the-classroom/.

Reflective Questions

- Are you explicitly planning to use the stories at your disposal as part of your teaching?
- How do you ensure that the more abstract elements of the past are tethered to pre-existing knowledge?
- Do you involve students in your thought processes when explaining the purpose of tasks?
- Are you successfully exploiting all available techniques in your explanations in order to make the concepts stick?

Chapter 3
Modelling

Ms Jensen's problematic source paper

Ms Jensen dreads the source-based units. Her students consistently perform strongly on the topics assessed by knowledge-based essays. She knows her stuff, explains and questions really well, and generally equips her students with good subject knowledge. Much of her unease seems unfounded as she has solid strategies to help students to draw sophisticated inferences, and they seem to understand the majority of the diary entries, posters, speeches and newspaper articles that she puts in front of them. However, despite her best attempts, she finds it nearly impossible to get her students to use these inferences and their contextual knowledge to answer the longer questions on the source paper. She gives students writing frames, with carefully planned structures, and shares plenty of exemplar answers gleaned from the exam board, but these don't appear to make the difference. Every time she takes in her Year 11 books she ends her marking session feeling frustrated as the answers she reads consistently misunderstand the focus of the question and fail to connect one idea to the next. Once again she worries that her students will be relying on paper one this year.

To use an analogy, if you wanted to teach someone how to cook a really great roast dinner you would not present them with the finished product and expect them to reproduce it having never witnessed its preparation. You would instead shepherd them through the process, at various points explaining and then demonstrating the importance of giving the potatoes a good shake after parboiling them, for example, or how to make sure you don't lose any of the flavour from the bottom of the roasting pan when making your gravy. To extend the metaphor a bit further – we will eventually get back to the history – you would not furnish your trainee cook with the knowledge necessary to produce the ultimate roast but never show them how those composite parts should be plated up together.

This, then, is how modelling fits into the process of teaching history. The history essay is our Sunday lunch and its mastery is similarly achieved through confidently bringing together a number of different elements to work in harmony. What these elements should include is the subject of substantial debate. We are often constrained by a mark scheme or descriptor of some shape or form and therefore often have to be led by this when deciding upon our ingredients. Michael Fordham has written fairly extensively on how we might move assessment forward and his message is that we should make this much more task-specific and rely less on generic descriptors with a set hierarchy of skills – for example, description, explanation, judgement.[1] In this way we could focus more on the particular knowledge associated with a time period rather than seeing history essay structures as essentially interchangeable no matter the topic. In

1 Michael Fordham, Levels: Where It All Went Wrong, *Clio Et Cetera* [blog] (8 February 2014). Available at: https://clioetcetera.com/2014/02/08/levels-where-is-all-went-wrong/.

practice, therefore, if you were studying the French Revolution, you would write assessment objectives specific to that period – including specific knowledge and understanding of the storming of the Bastille, for example, or of the concept of revolution – rather than falling back on generic descriptors focused on explanation. While this approach has substantial merit, it is not the purpose of this book to advocate a particular theory of assessment or curriculum, but rather to help all classroom teachers do the very best we can within the environment in which we find ourselves. However, the strategies that follow are more about process than specific outcomes, and would therefore be applicable to any format the history essay may take.

Modelling is effectively an extension of, and essential aid to, your explanation. It is the practice of moving the knowledge of abstract ideas in history, such as the causes of the Russian Revolution, towards concrete proof of this knowledge, as written on the page by our students. We aim to achieve this by helping students build their knowledge of the necessary elements of a finished piece of work, and of the connections and processes required to achieve it. So, not only will they be able to confidently tell you what Karl Marx's ideas were, but also to confidently write about them and connect them to the start of revolution in 1917. Historical writing is in this sense a discourse in its own right, a form of disciplinary knowledge that we must teach our students, linked to – but also separate from – the writing they do elsewhere. We need to recognise the peculiarities and particularities of historical writing and show our students how to replicate them.

Modelling does not start and finish with writing essays, however. It is inherent to everything we do; from our calm and courteous manner, to demonstrating how to fill in a table, to our thinking, to our care with presentation. As it is the written output that most often forms the ultimate conclusion to our study, this chapter will mostly focus on how modelling can be used to make this writing more successful, more often.

The number of different question styles that history students have to cope with can seem overwhelming, and we need to help them build confidence in their ability to tackle these. Modelling can be our best friend here. Breaking the components of answers down into manageable chunks and then demonstrating to students how to put those chunks back together is a skill to work on and refine. It can be intimidating at first – and if it is not something you are used to doing, be prepared for some false starts – but once your confidence builds it will become both natural and indispensable.

I can assure my past and present colleagues that Ms Jensen is wholly fictitious, but her problems echo a specific issue that departments I've been a part of have wrestled with: finding that the students consistently felt less confident with, and performed worse on, the source-based paper. Effective modelling can provide a solution, and this connects to something Rosenshine has referenced – that when taking students through a difficult task, modelling a procedure in small step-by-step chunks, followed by focused practice and repeating the cycle, is particularly effective.[2] Analysing the relative usefulness, reliability or similarity and difference of sources in essay format would undoubtedly fall into the bracket of a "difficult task". There are several factors at play; understanding the sources, understanding their context through detailed contextual knowledge of the time period, understanding the specific focus of the question, assessing the particular facet of the source that has been specified in the question, and then writing in a coherent and logical manner that communicates these various understandings. Added to this, the multi-levelled and, let's face it, often largely unintelligible mark schemes that accompany these questions do not make answering them any easier. To be clear, I am not suggesting we teach solely to satisfy a mark

2 Barak Rosenshine, Principles of Instruction: Research-Based Strategies That All Teachers Should Know, *American Educator*, 36(1) (2012): 12–19, 39. Available at: https://www.aft.org/sites/default/files/periodicals/Rosenshine.pdf.

scheme, indeed good historical discourse should always be our aim, but equally we cannot ignore these criteria entirely. Therefore, when we begin to support students in how best to tackle historical writing in its differing forms, we must know ourselves how to get from start to finish and be prepared to model each section first, and then the complete answer.

One universal truth in modelling is to respect the power of your whiteboard pen. PowerPoints have their place, and I use one to some extent in most lessons, but they also have their limitations. Using slides projected on a board with pre-typed answers that you've either written yourself or discovered elsewhere will not equip students with the tools necessary to write their own excellent responses, unless we incorporate them into a longer process of deconstruction and live modelling. We need to prove that the goal is achievable and demonstrate exactly how. This chapter predominantly promotes the use of strategies that require you to either write directly onto the whiteboard or to write over the top of what you are projecting. I've seen modelling done by teachers who are sat at a keyboard projecting what they are typing, but I wouldn't recommend it. The main reason is that you're not actually modelling what you want the students to do. They won't type their answers in the assessment or the exam, so until that changes I would stick with handwriting. A piece of *Blue Peter* style pre-made excellence is very much a part of this process but should be used as a starting point, not as a template to be simply distributed with the expectation that it is replicated by the students.

It is also worth noting that nothing exposes you quite like modelling. It can be a lonely place up at the front of the class when an answer starts to get away from you, or you inexplicably forget how to spell Lenin, or you confidently write that the British abolished the slave trade in 1933. However, the risk is worth the reward. As you practise you will develop a degree of automaticity – the ability to do something without actively concentrating on the actions or processes you are going through – and also refine the ability to effectively incorporate student responses into your writing and learn not to fear mistakes. Similar to challenge, this is a cultural shift in your classroom – and once the process of live modelling is well-established, any mistakes you do make will become useful signposts for the students as to where they might themselves trip up.

There are ways in which modelling can come up short, as many things look like modelling but fail to deliver the intended benefit. By missing out a step – for example, by asking students to compare model answers without first explaining and modelling what they need to look for – a well-intentioned activity can create more confusion than it alleviates. I am sure that almost all history teachers model to a greater or lesser extent already, so the following strategies are designed to help ensure that this modelling is effective and to build confidence in delivering it.

1. Model the Thinking

Before modelling how to write we should first model how to think about writing. Here we return to the principle of metacognition and how we must continually strive to develop our students' ability to think about the discipline of history in the way that we do. In order for students to develop their metacognitive abilities and to effectively plan, monitor and evaluate their learning, they need to possess three types of content knowledge: declarative, procedural and conditional.[3] Declarative knowledge is essentially facts – things you can say or declare are true – procedural knowledge is knowledge of how to perform a process step by step, and conditional knowledge is knowing when to use a procedure, skill or strategy and when not to use it. So, in history terms, declarative knowledge would be knowing that when Hitler makes a speech condemning communist actions on the night of 27 February 1933, he is talking about the Reichstag fire. Procedural knowledge would be having the necessary tools required to judge the usefulness of this speech by being able to comment effectively on the intended

3 William Peirce, Metacognition: Study Strategies, Monitoring, and Motivation (2003). Available at: http://academic.pg.cc.md.us/~wpeirce/MCCCTR/metacognition.htm.

audience, the purpose of the source and the information or detail that it does not include. Lastly, conditional knowledge would be understanding how to employ these analytical tools together, and how to combine the results to form a coherent extended answer that fully assesses the usefulness of the speech to Hitler's consolidation of power. Often you will find that students have the declarative knowledge and at least part of the necessary procedural knowledge but will fall down on the conditional component. This can be immensely frustrating and can lead to exasperated parents' evening comments such as, "She knows it verbally but she just can't get it down on the page," or to students telling us, "I don't know how to start," after which we patiently explain it to them for the fifth time.

A fix for this is to model the mental processes we would go through when encountering a tricky exam question by thinking out loud with the class:

Explain why William I was able to defeat rebellions between 1066 and 1070.

I would start by reading the question through once. I generally find that the first time I read a question it doesn't really sink in, so because of that, the next time I read it I always look for and think about the meaning of each of the words and phrases. This question starts with "explain why". Mike, what does that mean I've got to think of? Right, I now know that I've got to come up with some reasons, which are all about why something happened. So next I need to try to work out what knowledge I've got that will be useful. This particular question gives me a date range, "1066–1070", and a topic, "rebellions", so I'll make a quick note of any rebellions that happened in that time period. What other words give me a guide to the knowledge I'll need to include? That's correct, Millie, it mentions "defeat". What does that word mean in this context? I'm now trying to think of the main reasons why he was successful in dealing with the rebellions and to connect the question with my knowledge. Is there anything else that might be important in structuring my answer? Okay, it says "William" and "able to". That means I can assume that he was in fact successful and all I've got to do is prove why that was. Finally then, I'll work out the order in which to write my answer. I generally use chronology; it helps me connect one event to the next and stops me getting confused about what I'm writing about.

The difference between this approach and how I might have modelled before I looked into metacognition, is that previously I would have explained what the different parts of the question meant, probably alongside underlining key words, but I wouldn't have explicitly shared what I was thinking or the order in which I was thinking it. We must explicitly teach these thinking strategies if we want our students to employ them. Doing so can help our students avoid the damaging panic that can set in when reading an exam question, and save them minutes of inertia as they grapple with what to write and how to start. Once this modelling has been done live on the whiteboard several times you can then provide students with an entire past paper with all your thinking about the questions modelled via annotation. You can then get them to write their answers. Another strategy would be to give students tracing paper to cover past paper questions with, which they first annotate with their thinking before removing the tracing paper and completing the answers. This can be developed using the concept of spaced practice by leaving a few days between exploring the questions and answering them.

2. Thinking Through Sources

Metacognitive strategies are equally useful when developing students' ability to analyse sources. Annotating a source that is projected on your whiteboard with all the thoughts you have while trying to understand its meaning and relevance to a question is a perfect stepping stone to use when attempting to increase students' ability to tackle sources independently. Let's turn our attention to a source on Hitler's rise to power:

Hitler's official speech to the Reichstag on the Enabling Act, 23 March 1933

The burning of the Reichstag, one unsuccessful attempt within a large-scale operation, is only a taste of what Europe would have to expect from a triumph of this demonical doctrine. When a certain press, particularly outside Germany, today attempts, true to the political lie advanced to a principle by Communism, to link Germany's national uprising to this disgraceful act, this can only serve to strengthen my resolve to leave no stone unturned in order to avenge this crime as quickly as possible by having the guilty arsonist and his accomplices publicly executed! Neither the German Volk nor the rest of the world has become sufficiently conscious of the entire scope of the operation planned by this organization.[4]

I would model the following steps with the students, written as annotation over the source:

1. How I look at the question first, which directs me towards what to look for in the source itself.

4 Adolf Hitler, Official Speech on the Enabling Act to the Reichstag, Berlin, 23 March 1933. Available at: http://www.worldfuturefund.org/Reports2013/hitlerenablingact.htm.

2. How I deal with the provenance, applying my contextual knowledge to help me gain a feel for what tone and purpose the source is likely to have.
3. How I decode the content of the source, carefully cross-referencing details against my own knowledge.
4. What I would do if I didn't understand a particular word: blank it out, reread it and see if the context of the sentence still gives me some meaning I can use.

The focus is less on making specific inferences from this example and more about the general mechanisms of dealing with historical sources. Remember that this is a process you have done so many times that you probably do not notice yourself doing it. However, for students to replicate this, they need to be taught explicitly how. By doing this with a few example sources, it allows you to eventually skip some stages in your modelling when you annotate practice source questions as a class. Instead, you can ask the students to fill in the blanks as you think out loud: "What is the first thing I look at?" … "Why do I do that?"

3. Break it Down

The end goal of modelling will often be to lead the class through a jointly constructed extended answer with a number of different students contributing ideas, leading to a shared understanding of what makes the finished product excellent. However, before getting to this point it is important to break everything down, and model and give feedback on small sections of answers in order to build students' fluency with the composite parts that they need to master. Here you can use a pre-written answer, often referred to as a worked example and explained further in Strategy 4, and then model how it could be improved:

1. Show either a sentence, or several sentences, you have pre-written or select examples from the class that are in need of some improvement.
2. Write a tweaked version underneath the example, drawing students' attention to the changes you make and the thinking behind them.
3. Ask for student contributions about how it could be improved even further.
4. Repeat this process until you have an excellent sentence.
5. Ask students to practise writing their own sentences on the same topic.

If you were trying to teach your Key Stage 4 students how best to incorporate detailed and specific knowledge into their answers, the process could look like this:

Initial version: *"Highway robbery involved people stopping travellers and stealing their belongings. It was treated very seriously and the criminals got harsh punishments."*

First improvement: *"Highway robbery involved threatening or attacking travellers and forcing them to hand over valuable possessions. It was connected to the Bloody Code and the criminals got harsh punishments."*

Second improvement: *"Highway robbery involved threatening or attacking travellers and forcing them to hand over valuable possessions. It was connected to the Bloody Code, in which harsh punishments were used in order to deter criminals, meaning those caught could be given the death penalty."*

Third improvement: *"Highway robbery involved threatening or attacking travellers and forcing them to hand over valuable possessions. The crime carried the death penalty and was an example of the use of the Bloody Code, which saw capital punishment being used increasingly during the eighteenth century. From 1772, the use of capital punishment was extended to anyone found armed and in disguise on a high road."*

Each revision made is the result of several choices about knowledge and language. Judgements over both should be the subject of discussion and conjecture as the sentences grow and develop. Both the process and the end product are useful to the students, and once the culture of modelling in this way is embedded students will delight you as they pluck brilliant pieces of knowledge from their memories and find simple phrases to improve the writing.

4. Learn from the Best

Once you feel that your students are ready to tackle a complete piece of extended writing, sharing a pre-written answer that you have labelled – or that you label as a class – with the composite parts you have been working on is a good starting point. This benefits from what cognitive scientists refer to as the "worked example effect" – a worked example is a step-by-step demonstration of how to perform a task or how to solve a problem, which can be demonstrated by a completed piece of work.[5] By providing students with a pre-written answer you shrink their cognitive load by reducing the number of things that place demands on their limited working memory. This frees them up to focus on what they need to do, without having to think simultaneously about what the finished product will look like.

The example you use can be one you have written yourself, but more often I use an example from a previous year or from the class I'm teaching. The choice will depend on where in the learning cycle I'm using the model; if we haven't done much writing of this particular nature I will use work from a previous class taken from my portfolio of excellence, but as my current class gains proficiency I will use more examples of their work.

Picking examples from the class has the added benefit of building confidence in the fact that excellence is achievable. Knowing that the person sitting a few desks away wrote it rather than an exam board marker helps to convince students that they can produce something similar and can also build a useful bit of team spirit within the class. The answers you use don't have to represent perfection, just the best you could reasonably expect given the age of the students, time pressures and so on.

What I label will be specific to the objective of the essay. For example, for a causation question on the abolition of the slave trade with a Year 8 class, I would identify the specific knowledge being used – the evidence – and, separately, where that transitioned into directly answering the question – the explanation. This is often the part of the answer that students struggle most with, so identifying explicitly where it is done in an example will help them replicate it in their own writing. I may then use a third label to identify

5 Ruth C. Clark, Frank Nguyen and John Sweller, *Efficiency in Learning: Evidence-Based Guidelines to Manage Cognitive Load* (San Francisco, CA: Pfeiffer, 2006), p. 190.

additional layers of analysis, such as connecting one idea to another.

You could use a traditional structure to label the writing, such as point, evidence, explain (PEE). However, the problem here is that structures like this can communicate to students the idea that causation can be approached in the same way no matter the historical context and that their writing can follow a set structure, with the same phrases being used to start each section of their paragraphs no matter the topic. Each piece of history is distinct and the path of causation will be different. Therefore, focusing more on how the student has connected the events from cause to outcome for this topic in particular helps to create more accurate historical writing. To develop this idea further, I'll return to the nature of historical dialogue and discourse in Chapter 4.

For illustrative purposes, the worked example that follows, which has been adapted from my Year 8 portfolio of excellence and is far from perfect, uses straight underlining to identify the knowledge demonstrated and dotted underlining to identify where this directly or indirectly addresses causation. The dashed underlining is used to show where this has been connected to another idea.

A further reason slavery was abolished was because of the use of print media. People like Thomas Clarkson collected evidence against slavery. He spread his message by publishing essays and pamphlets as well as making speeches, which influenced many people. Furthermore, an ex-slave called Olaudah Equiano wrote a book of his story as a slave spreading the anti-slavery message. This contributed to slavery being abolished because this print media spread all over Britain and made people think twice about whether they should continue to support slavery. In this way key individuals were able to change public opinion and turn people against slavery.

The key here is to pick the example apart together. I find it useful to add a short problem-solving task such as: "Identify how many different pieces of knowledge are demonstrated in the paragraph by ticking each fact you find." As you get to know your class you can differentiate these tasks, depending on the specific aspects individuals or groups of students need to work on. Another common task I assign is to ask students to underline a particular key word each time they find it; in the example on page 65 it might be *abolition* or *slavery*. This is effective if you are attempting to direct their writing more precisely towards the question. You can also add to, revise and redraft the example together, writing directly onto a projection on the whiteboard.

One potential risk of this activity is that students who have struggled up to this point with extended writing will look at the worked example, panic and either literally or metaphorically throw their hands in the air and refuse to believe that something similar is within their capabilities. The important thing to stress with these students is that the example is designed to reveal the process they need to go through rather than to be directly copied or reproduced. You can then use scaffolds such as sentence starters to help them as needed.

5. Share the Load

Once the worked example has been picked apart and you are happy that your students can see what they are aiming for, start from scratch and co-create a model answer. This is the moment for a clean whiteboard, a new pen and a clear head. As mentioned previously, this does expose you as a teacher and if it has not been a part of your practice up to this point I would suggest building up to writing a whole answer rather than attempting it immediately in front of a class. Setting clear expectations is key and some of mine are: students always write with me (always stop to check that every student is writing the model down), contributions are given on my terms and students should expect to be questioned during the process.

The first time you model an answer it is sensible to do so without interruption; students will have enough to think about without also having to consider their contributions or answer questions. However, as you build students' confidence and familiarity with the creative process, you should start to include them in it. Ultimately you want to share the workload in the classroom. Without student involvement you will be doing all of the thinking, pouring your heart and soul into the answer while students switch to autopilot. Therefore, eventually sharing the burden with students is essential in modelling. This is the part our Ms Jensen was missing and the reason why her students were unable to bridge the gap between the examples they saw and the answers they wrote.

The sorts of questions you might pose to involve students could include:

- What words should I include in the first sentence of my answer?
- Where am I going to get my evidence from?
- How could I make that piece of evidence more precise?
- Which part of the source would be the most useful to include here?
- How do I now focus back on the question?

- What is the key word or phrase I've got to make sure I include?
- How can I connect these two important ideas?
- I'm not sure I have fully explained myself yet, so what could I include in the next sentence to ensure I do so?

Much of this can be pre-planned and you will find that as you model live more regularly you will develop the ability to balance encouraging student contributions with retaining control of the answer. Remembering to praise particularly pertinent contributions is important – and if you get a response that doesn't quite hit the mark, get another student to add to it and then combine the ideas to form something usable. These co-created pieces should be a springboard from which students can jump quickly into their own written answers, otherwise you can find that you lose some of the finer details you've covered. As you develop this practice you can add further layers to your models. I often use different colours in order to highlight different elements I want students to focus on. For example, in a usefulness answer I might use one colour to show where I use provenance and another for where I use contextual knowledge. I find this helps to deconstruct the different elements of a complex paragraph.

Reflective Questions

- Have you modelled your thinking about the question you are about to ask students to answer?
- How will you break an essay down into smaller chunks which you can model?
- How will you label your worked examples?
- Have you attempted to write a practice answer yourself from scratch?

- How will you ensure that students are part of the modelling process?
- How do you exemplify excellence?

Chapter 4
Practice

Edima's problems with practice

Another page in Edima's book has received an onslaught from her teacher's red pen. Dates, names and statistics have been corrected or added, and targets about how to structure her writing lie in wait at the bottom of her answer. Edima and her teacher share a crestfallen feeling as her book is handed back. Both had put substantial effort into the lessons that preceded this latest piece of writing. Each lesson was more exciting than the last, with every new piece of the historical jigsaw attacked with earnest endeavour. When reflecting on her work, Edima has the sense that she enjoyed those lessons. However, when it came to writing her essay on the topic, she encountered a couple of major problems. The main one was that she couldn't remember much of the detail from the lessons, just the general ideas. Also, without a clear idea of how to approach her answer, she had fallen back on how she had always written in the past. It seems that wasn't what her teacher was looking for on this occasion. This topic joins the growing number ticked as "not confident" on Edima's checklist.

Practice matters, in several different but connected ways. The first priority is simply devoting sufficient time to it. Rosenshine, in his seventeen principles of effective instruction, lists the following as point two:

Present new material in small steps, with student practice after each step.[1]

As history teachers we can be guilty of moving too quickly through, and sticking too rigidly to, the chronology that naturally guides our teaching. The reasons for this are manifest to anyone who studies or teaches the subject. To quote one of my all-time favourite Year 11 students, who will remain nameless, "You can't blag history, sir." To expand upon this eloquently put point, common sense and non-domain-specific knowledge will not fill in the gaps around the edges of most topics in history; you either know that particular part of the topic or you don't. This means that leaving even a small section of knowledge out of our teaching feels risky. So, we sit planning a series of lessons on the Tudors and agonise over which Acts of Uniformity we can afford to ignore. The effect of this is that we skip the practice and replace it with more new content. The problem this creates is that students do not get the essential opportunity, identified by Rosenshine, to work with newly encountered knowledge, understand it and store it for future use, as is the case for Edima. Without this opportunity students will struggle to remember the history we teach as it will simply sweep over them. Cognitive scientist Daniel Willingham estimates that, as a rule of thumb, students need to study a new concept for at least an additional 20% of the time it took them to master it in order to truly embed understanding and secure retention.[2] We need to guide and insist on this extra practice, as students are often a poor

---

1 Rosenshine, Principles of Instruction, p. 19.

2 Daniel T. Willingham, What Will Improve a Student's Memory?, *American Educator* (winter 2008–2009): 17–25, 44 at 22.

judge of their own fluency with a concept and will likely overestimate how much they will remember and, conversely, underestimate how much they will forget.

Therefore, if we are to overcome the tension of both doing justice to the rich history we deliver and giving students appropriate time to practise with it, then we need a plan. Much of this chapter is designed to develop teaching strategies and a curriculum with this in mind.

The second important consideration about practice focuses on the nature of it. As Doug Lemov and colleagues say in *Practice Perfect*, "practice makes permanent" rather than perfect.[3] Therefore, if students are given multiple opportunities to practise recalling their knowledge of the events leading up to the Berlin Blockade but when doing so are persistently labouring under the misconception that this refers to the Berlin Wall, then the misconception is what they'll remember. In this scenario the practice is actually damaging. That misconception will be really hard to dislodge and will pop up repeatedly like an unwanted weed. In this way practice is a thorny problem. The importance of doing it is undoubted, but the potential cost of getting it wrong is greater than with any of the other principles.

3 Doug Lemov, Erica Woolway and Katie Yezzi, *Practice Perfect: 42 Rules for Getting Better at Getting Better* (San Francisco, CA: Jossey-Bass, 2012), p. 3.

To develop our understanding of the nature of practice further, in *Making Every Lesson Count* Shaun and Andy proposed that we consider two distinct types of practice:

1. Practice for fluency – so that we achieve automaticity.
2. Deliberate practice, now more commonly called purposeful practice – so that we practise at the outer reaches of our ability.[4]

First, when it comes to fluency we are referring to knowledge and procedures so well-consolidated in a student's long-term memory that they can be recalled or performed effortlessly. In this way they will not impinge on the learner's working memory and cognitive load, allowing them to deal more successfully with the knowledge being encountered for the first time. Put another way, once students have mastered the concept of communism they will be able to recall its meaning without having to devote too much thought to it. This means that when they first encounter Ho Chi Minh and learn about his aims for Vietnam they will be able to concentrate on the new detail without the added confusion of exploring the context of his views. The secondary, but no less important, benefit is that he will intrinsically make more sense to them because they have already mastered the concept of communism. They can then tether his specific aims to their existing knowledge of the broad aims of communism and understand the roots of his intentions. He will make more sense to them because of their prior learning. As Willingham puts it, "We understand new things in the context of things we already know, and most of what we know is concrete."[5]

In Chapter 1 I referred to these key pieces of knowledge as Rosetta Stone concepts. So much of history is distinct, but there are concepts that drift across eras and, as with communism and Ho Chi Minh, once mastered can help to put the past in context and make it less of an alien landscape. The

4 Allison and Tharby, *Making Every Lesson Count*, pp. 126–127.
5 Willingham, *Why Don't Students Like School?*, p. 67.

generally accepted terminology to describe these is "substantive concepts". Michael Fordham ran a project to put together a list of these concepts for both Key Stage 2 and Key Stage 3 history.[6] The Key Stage 3 version is excellent and is included in full below:

Key Stage 3 Substantive Concepts

Absolute monarchy
Amendment[A]
Anarchism
Authority
Autocracy
Bill
Campaign[B]
Campaign[C]
Capitalism
Chivalry
Civil liberties
Civil Rights
Civil Servant
Civilian
Clan
Class
Cleric
Colonialism
Communism
Conservative
Constitution
Culture
Dictator
Free trade
Fundamentalism
Gentry
Heresy
Heretic
Hierarchy
Holy war
Illegitimacy
Imperialism
Industrialisation
Judicial Review
Judiciary
Legislative
Liberal
Liberty
Limited monarchy
Litigation
Manorial rights
Mercantilism
Middle Class
Minister
Minority[F]
Minority[G]
Propaganda
Protectionism
Racism
Radical
Recession
Reform
Regency
Regent
Resistance
Revolution
Royal court
Separation of powers
Skilled labourers
Socialism
Sovereignty
State
Suffrage
Tariff
Terrorism
Theocracy
Totalitarian
Trade union
Treaty

6 Michael Fordham, Substantive Concepts at KS2 & KS3, *Clio Et Cetera* [blog] (9 November 2017). Available at: https://clioetcetera.com/2017/11/09/substantive-concepts-at-ks2-ks3/.

Doctrine	Nationalism	Tyranny
Domestic policy	Papacy	Usurper
Duchy	Parliament	Working Class
Earldom	Patriarch	
Economic sanction	Patriot	
Estate[D]	Persecution	
Executive[E]	Pilgrimage	
Fascism	Populism	
Federal	President	
Feminism	Pretender	
Feudal	Prime Minister	
Foreign policy	Primogeniture	
	Principality	

A constitutional
B election
C military
D social class
E branch of government
F age
G government

This then comes back to the idea of the curriculum as the foundation of everything we do. If we accept that mastery of this list of substantive concepts would help our students across whatever combination of topics we choose to teach at Key Stage 3 – and by natural extension Key Stage 4 – we then need to construct a curriculum that is conducive to regular practice of these concepts. This would need to be multi-pronged and go beyond simply learning the definition of each word. As Fordham says, the meaning of these concepts shifts depending on the topic they are being applied to – for example, the concept of *estate* would have a different meaning depending on whether you encountered it through the French Revolution or industrial Britain.

This chapter focuses on the specific teaching strategies that could be employed to develop successful practice with these concepts. As a quick introductory overview you might want to use some of the following approaches, which will be more or less easy to action depending on your seniority within your team:

- Decide which concepts from the list fit best with your chosen curriculum and add any that, through discussion with colleagues, you have decided are indispensable. The list provided is not exhaustive, and, as with all resources of this type, should be tailored to your context.
- Unpick the concepts as a team. If you've got a medieval specialist, get them to lead on these concepts; if you have someone who loves the world wars, do likewise. It is essential that your team has a shared understanding in order to give your students one. This could be done as part of INSET or in a series of meetings.
- Get the concepts onto your knowledge organisers (see Strategy 1).
- Teach the concepts explicitly the first few times you encounter them. Do not expect students to learn them outside of the lesson as homework. For fluency to develop they must understand them deeply.
- Once taught explicitly, plan for how and when the concepts will be regularly returned to. Homework will play a part here.
- Decide how they will be highlighted within lessons. You could use a particular image to accompany them whenever they appear on a PowerPoint, or use a particular phrase when you encounter one – for example, "This links to one of our Rosetta Stone concepts: revolution."
- Think about your classroom displays and how you could incorporate the concepts into them.

The other element for us to consider is purposeful practice. This is perhaps the more concrete side of how our students practise in lessons. This is how we stretch and challenge our students and push them to the outer reaches of their capability. In doing so, we develop their ability to use what we teach them without our input. The subtlety with purposeful practice lies in knowing how much involvement to have with it as the teacher. This is shown by the continuum on page 79.[7]

Knowing where you are on this continuum is dependent on the class and the individuals you are teaching, as well as on the topic. Through experience you might know that you can release your grip sooner when attempting to build knowledge and understanding of Mary I's approach to heretics as opposed to Elizabeth I's approach to the poor. Additionally, your methods would be different for an Evie compared to an Edima.

There is also a further division of purposeful practice in history: how we develop students' competence with the knowledge we teach them and how we aid their historical writing. The two are interdependent but do not necessarily develop proportionally or congruently in all learners. We can all picture the student who can confidently tell us all about the four humours in ancient Greek medicine, but ask them to write a paragraph of explanation and it will appear that they have only the flimsiest understanding. Equally, we encounter students who write in exactly the manner we require but consistently demonstrate a lack of conceptual understanding of the history they are writing about. Logically, the chronology of purposeful practice has three stages in history:

1. **Practise with the knowledge by rehearsing and testing it.** For example, work through the causes, key features and consequences of the Berlin Blockade. Focus on common misconceptions, such as confusion with the Berlin Wall and the position of Berlin behind the Iron Curtain.

2. **Practise critical thinking by rolling our new knowledge around and forming opinions and judgements.** For example, who was to blame for the blockade beginning? Why was this different to all the events in the

---

7 This first appeared in Allison and Tharby, *Making Every Lesson Count*, p. 128.

Dependence	Heavy guidance	Light guidance	Independence	Autonomy
Teacher explains and models new content. Students are predominantly listening, watching and taking notes.	Teacher leads practice through questioning, discussion and supports. Cognitive work is shared with the teacher.	Students are doing cognitive work on their own with regular teacher feedback and fewer supports.	Students work with and apply new knowledge for an extended period of time without the teacher's support. All cognitive work has now been passed to the student.	Students fluently manipulate knowledge and skills independently by applying them to new contexts.

Cold War up to this point? Why was Berlin always destined to be a Cold War flashpoint? Why was the world a more dangerous place after the blockade ended?

3 **Practise applying the knowledge through writing.** For example, explain why Stalin began the blockade of Berlin in 1948. Write a narrative account of the Berlin Blockade. Explain two consequences of the Berlin Blockade.

Any debate around practising knowledge and critical thinking will largely be around the most effective methods of doing so; perhaps over the quantity of these tasks, their frequency, the amount of direct instruction involved, and so on. However, when it comes to writing in history the debate is more nuanced. The tension, as always, is in balancing how far we teach students to write a historical discourse that we value as subject specialists against how far we teach them to write in a manner that we recognise as being most likely to secure them high marks on whatever externally marked assessment they are beholden to. This is the subject of some really interesting conversations between history teachers.

Most departments that I have worked in or with have shared writing structures, sentence starters or connectives with their students in some shape or form. These are created for legitimate and understandable reasons, and are generally shared to help students meet certain assessment objectives, set either internally or externally. They provide students with a roadmap to follow as they navigate their way through an answer, and I've seen them used effectively to shape an incoherent writer into a disciplined one.

However, over the last decade or so, leading thinkers and writers in the world of history teaching – including Christine Counsell and James Woodcock – have rightfully questioned the wisdom of encouraging our students to fit their writing around generic structures. To summarise the argument, we should think judiciously about the sentence starters we share, as some, while potentially meeting an assessment objective, may inhibit good historical writing.

Teacher Jim Carroll has written some really excellent articles and blog posts in this area, and has suggested some ways in which we might increase the correlation between how historians write and how history students do. One example that particularly resonated with me was his suggestion that by teaching students certain generic language to use when writing causation essays, we may in fact be damaging their historical discourse.[8] This built on the work of James Woodcock, who argued that by giving students a deeper understanding of specific vocabulary we could help them develop more precise and nuanced responses to causation questions.[9]

An idea that both Jim and James propose is that the best causational explanation uses domain-specific or disciplinary language and knowledge rather than generic connective phrases. Jim used the following examples to illustrate the difference between how students might write about the causes of the Salem witch hunt and how historian Enders A. Robinson has:

Example 1, using the traditional format of generic causational connective phrases:

Puritan leaders were worried that people in New England were becoming less devout, which **led to** *powerful male leaders in Massachusetts looking for scapegoats.* **Consequently,** *these leaders' anxiety* **meant** *they were willing to listen to the girls' accusations which* **caused** *the Salem witch hunt.*

---

8 Jim Carroll, Duplo to Watercolours: How the Substantive Might Shape the Disciplinary in Students' Historical Causal Arguments, *J Carroll History* [blog] (2 March 2018). Available at: https://jcarrollhistory.com/2018/03/02/duplo-to-watercolours-how-the-substantive-might-shape-the-disciplinary-in-students-causal-arguments/.

9 James Woodcock, Does the Linguistic Release the Conceptual? Helping Year 10 to Improve Their Causal Reasoning, *Teaching History*, 119 (2005): 5–14.

Example 2, using disciplinary knowledge to drive the explanation of causation:

At the strategic level, the old-guard Puritans **granted the authority under which** *the conspiracies operated. The beginning of 1692 saw the old guard running an outlaw government in New England, these men were the councillors, magistrates, judges, and high military officers. Only the old guard had sufficient authority* **to sanction** *the atrocities of the witch hunt.*

Jim admits that the first example is perfectly good, but as a piece of historical discourse the second is clearly better. I find it hard to argue with that judgement.

I'm not suggesting that when we enter our classrooms on Monday we immediately abandon all connective mats, or order Year 7 to tear down our displays of sentence starters, or declare to our department that all our students' writing up to this point has been deeply flawed. Pragmatism in teaching is normal, natural and often necessary, and writing scaffolds are certainly pragmatic. However, at points we should put the external pressures to one side and allow a bit of idealism to enter our thinking.

We could use the two examples about the Salem witch hunts as a practical way to extend our most able. For those students, constraining or confining them to using scaffolds when they practise may in fact be putting unhelpful straightjackets on their writing. Using example 2, we could demonstrate that knowledge and explanation are intrinsically linked – rather than intrinsically separate – and help them to weave the two together in the way that the best historical discourse does. However, for many other students, example 1 might be an excellent outcome that has taken weeks of careful scaffolding and practice to produce.

1. Knowledge Organisers

An excellent starting point is to get all of the knowledge you want students to practise with in one place. Knowledge organisers are a very practical way of doing this. They essentially create a single reference point for all the vital information on a particular topic. The exact origin of the knowledge organisers concept is hard to find. They are one of those strategies that benefitted from a buzz across the educational Twitter world, which for the uninitiated is a useful, although sometimes infuriating, place to read about new thinking and source ideas.

Knowledge-based curricula have been more in vogue recently and are perhaps best represented by Michaela Community School, which champions both a knowledge-based curriculum and teaching approach. Former Michaela teacher Joe Kirby wrote a blog post about knowledge organisers back in 2015 which neatly summarised the value of specifying and sequencing details such as dates, events, characters, concepts and precise definitions.[10]

For some subjects, such as English literature, knowledge organisers can be quite a departure as the subject has not traditionally been taught as knowledge-based and therefore this feels like a shift to something new. However, us history teachers have always used crib sheets of some kind or another, and accept that there are defined pieces of knowledge within our subject that we need our students to know. Therefore, knowledge organisers may not feel like anything particularly groundbreaking. Added to this, if they are poorly conceived or underused then they will be more of a source of confusion than assistance. However, I've been using them for a while now and have found them really useful. In order to get them right there are two key elements to consider: first, their design, and second, their use.

In terms of design I would recommend creating your own. There are a myriad available online and by all means take these as a starting point, but you will find them much easier to use with your students if you invest the time to make them yourself. As a department, we have been through several drafts of the ones we use with our Key Stage 4 students, which unfortunately are too bulky to include in full in this book, and as I've said, it is always advantageous to customise them to your needs. So, here are some tips for how to create and use them based on my experience:

- Agree the content and look at it as a department. At Key Stage 3, a substantive concepts list would be a good place to start and for older students exam specifications and questions will certainly play a part, although do not ignore your own experience and priorities.
- Include the key components of a good history knowledge organiser, which are:

10 Joe Kirby, Knowledge Organisers, *Pragmatic Education* [blog] (28 March 2015). Available at: https://pragmaticreform.wordpress.com/2015/03/28/knowledge-organisers/.

- ◊ A timeline of key events, if possible accompanied by a short description of each.
- ◊ A glossary of tier 3 vocabulary with definitions.
- ◊ A glossary of tier 2 vocabulary with history-specific definitions – these may come from exam questions.
- ◊ Mini biographies of key individuals with descriptions.
- ◊ A relevant and memorable image where possible.

- ♦ Pare down the knowledge as far as possible and organise it under clear headings. It is tempting to overload knowledge organisers and end up with a sea of size 7 font. This is likely to terrify students and therefore be less useful in the long run. If you feel you can't get enough detail on to your knowledge organiser, make separate ones to cover specific areas.
- ♦ Get them stuck into students' books and accessible on whatever online system your school uses. You can also have extra hard copies available on a display board for students to grab.
- ♦ Refer to them regularly when teaching. When you use a piece of tier 3 vocabulary, say, "You will find that word on your knowledge organiser – can someone tell me the definition, please?"
- ♦ Explicitly teach the content rather than expecting students to learn it independently from the knowledge organiser. Use the knowledge organiser as you do so, but the key rule of thumb should be that students do not have to understand anything on there before you have explained it first.
- ♦ Use them for homework. This could involve preparing for an assessment or a quiz and should be accompanied by instructions on how to use the knowledge organiser in this context – for example, to make a mind map of the first five events on the timeline. Towards the end of the

topic, hand out a pared-down copy of the knowledge organiser, with only the headings included, for students to complete from memory.

- Use them for revision. Create packs of them to cover different topics as students prepare for exams. These feel personal to the students and they will value them more than the standard revision guide.
- After completing an extended piece of writing, ask students to read back through their work and highlight each mention of a term or person included on the knowledge organiser. This is a really purposeful whole-class redrafting activity.
- Do not forget about them. If you do not prioritise knowledge organisers, emphasise their importance and refer to them regularly, they will become just another piece of paper that students ignore.

2. Checklists

These can be used in tandem with your knowledge organisers and are a way for students to monitor their own areas of strength and weakness. As with knowledge organisers there are multiple examples available online, but contrary to my previous advice these can often be plug and play if you find a good one. These do not contain specific information about the topics – you may find some that do, but if using in conjunction with a knowledge organiser it makes sense if your checklist doesn't – and are instead used for students to self-monitor their fluency with topics as a year or key stage progresses. Here are a few tips for making or using them in history:

- Look to chunk the subject matter down as precisely as possible. If you leave any room for interpretation as to what topic you mean, or if the topic listed is too broad and encompasses several smaller themes, then there is the potential for students to develop false confidence in what they know.

- Check the vocabulary against what you use in class and in any other learning materials. It should dovetail to avoid misunderstanding.
- Include them in any revision packs you create.
- Include them at the start of lessons so students know where the lesson fits into the overall topic.
- Use them as a metacognitive strategy. Students can colour them red, amber or green according to their fluency with each topic.
- Use them to help students identify any topics they have missed through absence.

3. Retrieval Practice

This strategy is so important it's almost deserving of its own chapter, and if this book was in colour this section would be written in bright orange to make it stand out. It would be fair to say that an understanding of the principle and importance of retrieval practice, and the evidence base behind it, has had a transformational effect on my teaching practice. The principle is prioritised by cognitive scientist John Dunlosky as one of the most important strategies that teachers can apply in their classrooms.[11] He explains that there is a huge weight of evidence to support the importance of students recalling information from their long-term memory to enhance and secure learning.

Essentially, retrieval practice involves students bringing knowledge, concepts or procedures from their long-term memory back into their working memory. This process of retrieval strengthens the memory and the more it is repeated, the more embedded the memory will become – and, therefore, more accessible for future use. This has been proven to be an incredibly powerful method of improving memory and learning. There won't be a history teacher reading this book who has not, in some form or another, used retrieval practice when teaching, be that a few verbal questions at the start of a lesson, a hastily concocted quiz or something far more regimented and structured. However, for this strategy to have the transformational effect it is capable of on students' ability to retain and recall the history we have taught them, it needs to be an inherent part of our curriculum, assessment and teaching.

In order to support this I've split the strategy into two parts: first, the principles to stick to when applying it in history, and second, practical ways of incorporating it into your teaching. The principles are as follows:

- **Build in forgetting time.** Simply testing what you have learnt that lesson does not support long-term retention. You should test recall of information learnt last lesson, last month and last year.
- **Make it habitual.** If you leave incorporating it into your lessons to chance then you'll neglect it more than you

11 Dunlosky, Strengthening the Student Toolbox, p. 13.

should. This will take a fair bit of heavy lifting in the early stages but will be worth it in the long run.

- **Think carefully about what you are testing.** Make sure you've identified the most useful bits of knowledge to repetitively test. If not you'll be arming students with only some of what they'll need.
- **Interleave topics.** This is the principle of alternating between different topics when you study them and is another of the Learning Scientists' six strategies.[12] For me it doesn't fit well with general history teaching, which tends to benefit from a chronological approach, but is great for retrieval practice. First, two questions from topic 1; next, a couple from topic 2 and so on.
- **Give immediate feedback.** If you fail to correct misconceptions straight away then these will become embedded. Therefore, always give the correct answers immediately after questioning.
- **Make it low stakes.** Try to alleviate anxiety around the results of any quizzing that you do. Research shows that the act of testing actually supports later retention; therefore, the important thing is for students to test their recall, not to fixate on how many they get right.[13]

We can put the principles into practice using the following strategies:

- **Write 100 questions for every topic you teach.** This is a starting point that can be adapted into a thousand different resources. Make sure you include all the answers as well! This might sound obvious but if you don't then there is the more room for inconsistency and misconception.

---

12 Smith and Weinstein, Six Strategies for Effective Learning.

13 Henry L. Roediger III, Adam L. Putnam and Megan A. Smith, Ten Benefits of Testing and Their Applications to Educational Practice. In Jose P. Mestre and Brian H. Ross (eds), *The Psychology of Learning and Motivation, Volume 55: Cognition in Education* (San Diego, CA: Elsevier Academic Press, 2011), pp. 1–36. Available at: http://dx.doi.org/10.1016/B978-0-12-387691-1.00001-6.

- **Trigger words.** This is an alternative form of retrieval practice which involves reducing a topic to a few key words or phrases designed to trigger memories. Students then elaborate on these, either by writing down all they can remember or by turning them into a mind map. The following example is for the Prague Spring:

Czechoslovakia, 1968

Opposition	Human face
Brezhnev	Warsaw Pact
500,000	Doctrine

- **Mind maps from memory.** Give students a key question and a few topic headings and let them do the rest.
- **Timelines from memory.** Give students a topic and a start and finish date and then ask them to fill in any events that they can remember. Do this using one colour pen, then allow them to check their notes and add to or correct their timeline using a different colour.
- **Blank knowledge organisers.** Provide the headings and ask the students to fill in the detail.
- **Challenge grids.** Teacher Kate Jones has developed an excellent retrieval practice strategy that she refers to as challenge grids.[14] This is a question grid with a variable number of points available for each correct answer. Questions are assigned 1 to 4 points, with more points available for recalling the knowledge learnt longest ago.
- **Recall with no notes in sight.** Retrieval practice must be done from memory. Also try to prevent students from quickly checking back in their notes before you do a quiz.

---

14 Kate Jones, Retrieval Practice Challenge Grids for the Classroom, *Love to Teach* [blog] (12 January 2018). Available at: https://lovetoteach87.com/2018/01/12/retrieval-practice-challenge-grids-for-the-classroom/.

- **Start with the practice.** If you use generic PowerPoints for your schemes of work then put a retrieval practice slide at the start. Ideally this will be complete with questions that students will answer straight away, but initially this might just be a prompt to dip into questioning.
- **Keep it low stakes.** To make it feel more relaxed and less like formal assessment, allow students to mark their own answers.
- **Check understanding.** Also on the low stakes theme, to check general understanding ask, "Who got this one right?" Students will be happier to put their hand up for this as opposed to, "Who got more than five right?" It also allows you to see which specific pieces of knowledge were more commonly recalled and which areas need additional focus.
- **Make it integral to homework.** All homework should include some form of retrieval practice.
- **Prioritise it as a revision strategy.** Flashcards are a great approach. However, make sure you model how to create one with the question on one side and the answer on the other. If not, you may find students just rewrite notes onto small bits of card.

4. Present it Differently

To aid the retention of new knowledge, aim to present it in a variety of different ways the first time you teach it. In *The Hidden Lives of Learners*, Graham Nuthall revealed that to secure a new concept a learner must encounter it at least three times, and preferably more.[15] Therefore, we should use this as a rule of thumb when teaching. As mentioned previously, the first method will almost certainly be your own explanation. However, don't be afraid to add a bit of repetition by finding alternative ways to communicate the details of the historical event you are introducing. To exemplify this, if you were teaching First World War trench life for the first time, you could use the following sources:

- A short video clip from a documentary of your choosing.
- A newsreel clip. British Pathé has an excellent bank of these.[16]

15 Graham Nuthall, *The Hidden Lives of Learners* (Wellington: New Zealand Council for Educational Research Press, 2007), p. 127.

16 See https://www.britishpathe.com/workspaces/page/ww1-the-definitive-collection.

- A relevant section from the textbook.
- First-hand accounts from soldiers.
- Photos, paintings or drawings.
- Historians' interpretations.
- Political cartoons.
- Newspaper reports, which would need contextualising due to the impact of censorship under the Defence of the Realm Act on reporting.

I would select two from this list to supplement my own explanation. Whichever combination you choose it is always worth asking yourself how each element will contribute to students' knowledge and understanding. I am of the opinion that history is engaging enough in itself when taught passionately, and so is not in need of what might be termed artificial support. Therefore, if you are planning role play or something similar to explore a new topic, always ask yourself, will this work better than if I just told them about it or they read about it?

5. Practise Thinking Hard

Once you've practised learning the knowledge, you then need to practise thinking about it. This would be stage two in the three stages of purposeful practice, in which we take the content and begin to form critical judgements about it. In Chapter 1, I referred to using a timeline as a living graph, which is an excellent example of an activity that is designed to elicit deeper thinking in history. This is the type of activity I would recommend at this stage. You have transmitted the essential knowledge and now you need to roll that knowledge around and help students form judgements and opinions. Try to avoid long periods of low challenge activities that occupy but do not stretch thinking. So, before embarking on that cut and stick timeline, ask yourself whether students will be learning the chronology or improving the accuracy of their scissor skills. The chunks of the lesson in which students grapple with knowledge should contain a problem-solving element to deepen thinking. Some suggested activities would be:

- **Diamond 9s.** Ask the students to prioritise factors by organising nine key points into the shape of diamond: the one at the top is the most important and the one at the bottom is least important. The sequence settled upon then needs unpicking with questioning.
- **Concept maps.** Students dot pieces of new knowledge around a blank piece of paper and then try to connect them in whatever way they can. They can draw circles of differing sizes around the factors to denote their relative importance; the larger the circle, the greater the significance.
- **Continuums.** Students place the chunks of knowledge or historical sources they are working with onto a continuum. This could be framed against a statement, with "Agree" and "Disagree" at each end of the continuum.
- **Card sorts.** I often use numbered boxes and then do the reordering with the numbers rather than writing out long sentences or cutting and sticking.
- **Use word limits.** Ask students to convert a lengthy piece of text about their new learning into a sentence of no more than thirty words. Asking them to be concise ensures they think about what is of critical importance.
- **Elaborate.** Ask students to come up with questions of their own about a topic. There needs to be some modelling and scaffolding here to avoid pointless questions.

6. Create the Culture

In order for practice to work well you need to build a classroom culture which is conducive to it. The vast majority of students will gravitate towards the social norms that exist in your classroom, so these need to facilitate good practice. Here are some ideas for establishing this:

- **Limit the distractions.** As mentioned previously, our working memory is limited, so anything that adds to cognitive load will inhibit learning. Therefore, the more distractions that exist in your classroom, the harder it will be for students to practise effectively. Often we can be the biggest distraction, feeling the need to break the silence or to talk authoritatively about something that has just occurred to us while students are trying to work.
- **Encourage struggle.** As per Professor Coe's three questions (see page 11), we must encourage students to struggle and make it the expectation in our classrooms.
- **Know when to stay put.** History teacher Ben Newmark wrote a really good blog post about how we as teachers have learnt to be scared to stay at our desks.[17] However, often this is absolutely the right thing to do as it communicates trust and helps to send a signal that this is the time for students to get their heads down and get on.
- **Find the bright spots.** Make a big show of highlighting excellent work being done in the class. This could be done verbally or even electronically, by taking a photo on your phone and projecting it onto your whiteboard.
- **Set rules and stick to them.** From the moment you first set eyes on your class make it clear what your expectations are on effort and presentation when practising. If they break them, make sure the sanctions follow.

---

17 Ben Newmark, Am I Allowed to Sit at My Desk?, *BENNEWMARK* [blog] (16 February 2018). Available at: https://bennewmark.wordpress.com/2018/02/16/am-i-allowed-to-sit-at-my-desk/.

- **No space to hide.** By the time they get to you, some students may have become very skilled at hiding a lack of effort. You need to know who those students are and nudge them regularly.

7. Scaffold

As already discussed, the creation of effective extended writing in history is a complex process. It is the method of analysis and thought that we measure, and the conduit for expression within our discipline. History books are beautiful things and show off the ultimate end point that the embryonic versions of historical discourse produced within our classrooms are aiming for. As teachers we have likely all struggled through the process of how to write a good history essay and can probably remember our own dissertations being pulled apart at various times.

We need to support our students with this struggle and scaffolding their writing is an integral part of this. The metaphor refers to the manner in which we construct supports around their writing and then remove these at the right time. Knowing when and how to do this will be dependent upon the student and is ultimately the main form of differentiation that I would promote.

So how can we scaffold effectively?

- **Model first.** Before the scaffold should come the modelling, as this will allow students to see the process.
- **Sentence starters and structures.** As discussed previously, these are to be used judiciously and at their best should stimulate thinking and expression rather than stifle it. Avoid using the same sentence starters across all essay types and topics. Make them as specific to the content as possible and avoid generic structures that will constrain students. Also, try to design sentence starters

that make statements rather than give unsubstantiated opinions, so, "Ultimately, this led to … because …" rather than, "I think that this happened because …" In this way we bring their writing closer to the history books we love. Don't inadvertently teach students to apply set sentence starters to answer specific questions; rather, give a basic structure and suggested language they can use to fit each part of the structure. A list of useful phrases, not necessarily starters, that would apply to an essay focused on consequence would be:

Which resulted in

Which led to

As a result of this

Played an essential role in

Directly affected

Consequently

Had a decisive effect on

- **Use your knowledge organisers.** These can be used to scaffold writing by helping students select key terminology to include.
- **Intervene.** Some students will need robust scaffolding and some will just need a nudge. For some students, physically writing out the start of their sentences will be necessary, while for others you can offer suggestions verbally. Equally, a simple tap on the table will be enough to get some students on task, while for others a short elaboration question, written on their work as you read over their shoulder, will help refocus their writing.
- **Chunk it up.** As you build towards students writing a full essay independently you will need to break it up first. You can do this in stages, first providing an opportunity to write a scaffolded main body paragraph and then, separately, a scaffolded conclusion. If you give a detailed, full-answer scaffold covering all the points you would

include in your ideal essay, you will probably find that the students are filling in the blanks of your thinking rather than doing much of their own.

- **Scaffold a plan.** If you can get this right then your scaffolds for writing will drop away more quickly.
- **Remove the scaffolds.** Ultimately, we should aim to take the stabilisers off, allowing our students to work unencumbered by restriction. This should always be the aim of the scaffolds we use but, in my experience, often it is not. Again, when and how to do this will be specific to the student, and is not exclusive to the more able. For our lower ability students, paragraph structures can seem hugely daunting, so asking them to write their answer "as they would say it" can be more effective.

Reflective Questions

- Are you giving students enough time to practise with new material?
- Are students practising at the limit of their capabilities?
- Have you defined the knowledge you want your students to practise with?
- Have you created a classroom culture that is conducive to practice?
- Have you created scaffolds that stimulate thinking?

Chapter 5
Feedback

All work and no impact makes Mr Tremblay an unhappy teacher

A nagging feeling is starting to accompany every marking session Mr Tremblay does. It has been there for some time and is getting harder to ignore. He dutifully follows his department's policy, which requires him to give written feedback on a piece of extended writing every two weeks. His students have been practising causation essays recently, and, while the marking is tiresome, he works through it as he is keen for his students to improve. However, increasingly, Mr Tremblay is questioning the impact that his marking is having. He wonders about the connection between the difficulty many students are having with linking the cause to the outcome, the comments he is writing and his students' ability to do better next time. The targets he writes are specific to each student and take cues from the assessment objectives which are identified by the accompanying mark scheme. However, as he circulates the class while his students work on redrafting their answers, he notices that the majority of these are filled with the same misconceptions and undeveloped explanations as the originals. Mr Tremblay looks to the ceiling tiles and sighs.

The benefit of giving students good, timely feedback has a substantial weight of research evidence behind it. The EEF Teaching and Learning Toolkit ranks it alongside metacognition and self-regulation as the strand that has the strongest effect on learning.[1] A problem for history teachers is that the connection between learning and feedback is often misinterpreted as a connection between learning and marking. It is essential that we do not conflate the two; feedback and marking are not the same.

The effect sizes graph from John Hattie's meta-analysis of thousands of studies has been shown at INSETs up and down the country over the past couple of years, usually with a little red circle hovering over feedback to emphasise its importance.[2] As with other sources of evidence in this area, it shows that good feedback has a hugely beneficial effect on learning; the graphic shows feedback as having an effect size of 0.73, and anything over 0.4 is considered good.

We tend to hear feedback and think marking. However, neither the EEF's toolkit nor Hattie's meta-analysis suggest that feedback necessarily needs to be in this form. Here, then, is the rub. Armed with this misconception, history departments go away and write feedback policies that are in fact marking policies, and burden teachers with expectations that push us to our workload limits. The reason why we, as history teachers or leaders of history, must be so careful with this approach to feedback is because – alongside English – our subject sees the greatest production of extended writing in school. The simple maths of this means that the time commitment required to provide written feedback on a set of history essays is huge.

Now, the devil, as always, lies in the detail. Mr Tremblay's marking is ineffective and, as a result, largely a waste of his

---

1 See https://educationendowmentfoundation.org.uk/evidence-summaries/teaching-learning-toolkit/feedback/.

2 See Sebastian Waack, Hattie Ranking: Backup of 138 Effects Related to Student Achievement, *Visible Learning* [blog] (2016). Available at: https://visible-learning.org/2016/04/hattie-ranking-backup-of-138-effects/.

time because the students cannot interpret it in a manner that allows them to enact change. In fact, in the same way that good feedback has a marked positive effect on learning, bad feedback has a proportional negative effect. Therefore, if you get feedback wrong you could actually damage student learning and may have been better not giving any at all. It seems Mr Tremblay may not be alone; a powerful piece of evidence comes from a meta-analysis by Kluger and DeNisi in which 38% of the studies examined indicated that feedback actually had negative effects.[3]

However – before you bin your red pens – it is important to remember that not all marking in history is ineffective, and I would certainly advocate it being part of the feedback tapestry that we look to weave with our classes. We just need to be precise and judicious in how we use it. It is hard to find concrete guidance on written feedback as the jury is still out on its overall impact. However, a report commissioned by the EEF recommended the following, while also recognising the lack of conclusive evidence on the matter:

- *Careless mistakes should be marked differently to errors resulting from misunderstanding. The latter may be best addressed by providing hints or questions which lead pupils to underlying principles; the former by simply marking the mistake as incorrect, without giving the right answer.*
- *Awarding grades for every piece of work may reduce the impact of marking, particularly if pupils become preoccupied with grades at the expense of a consideration of teachers' formative comments.*
- *The use of targets to make marking as specific and actionable as possible is likely to increase pupil progress.*

3 Avraham N. Kluger and Angelo DeNisi, The Effects of Feedback Interventions on Performance: A Historical Review, a Meta-Analysis, and a Preliminary Feedback Intervention Theory, *Psychological Bulletin*, 119(2) (1996): 254–284 at p. 258.

- *Pupils are unlikely to benefit from marking unless some time is set aside to enable pupils to consider and respond to marking.*
- *Some forms of marking, including acknowledgement marking, are unlikely to enhance pupil progress. A mantra might be that schools should mark less in terms of the number of pieces of work marked, but mark better.*[4]

These seem like sensible principles on which to base an approach to marking, and several of the strategies in this chapter will aim to interpret these for history. However, there are a wide variety of opportunities for feedback in history lessons that go beyond traditional marking. Most are led by the teacher and could include: adaptations to teaching, whole-class feedback, individual verbal feedback and live marking. Others can be driven by students through, for example, self-reflection or peer feedback. Each of these strategies has its own principles to follow – and potential pitfalls – and, taken together with marking, should form part of your composite collection of approaches to feedback. By both recognising the value of the feedback we already give and widening the variety of the feedback strategies we routinely employ, we can have a dramatic effect on our workload while not diminishing feedback's vital importance.

Feedback ultimately has four main roles: to show students what they need to aim for; to keep them on track; to let them know whether they have got there or not; and to point them in the direction of their next goal. The central tenet of all feedback is that it should be a reciprocal process. It should not be seen as something we simply deliver as teachers, rather as a process in which information is passed back and forth between teacher and student. This is exemplified in the following diagram:

4 Victoria Elliott et al., *A Marked Improvement? A Review of the Evidence on Written Marking* (London: Education Endowment Foundation, 2016). Available at: https://educationendowmentfoundation.org.uk/public/files/Publications/EEF_Marking_Review_April_2016.pdf, p. 5.

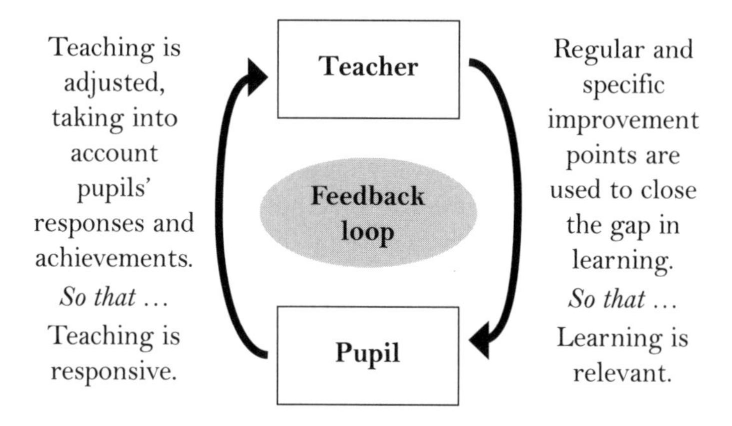

As teachers we identify each student's "learning gap" – something they cannot yet do or do not yet know – and then provide feedback aimed at closing that gap. The feedback we get from students in return helps us to know exactly how to plug that gap and what with. For example, students might be writing a short essay about the causes of the English Reformation. As you read over their shoulders, you notice that as a class they have consistently failed to include anything about the origins of the new Protestant religion. After they finish their responses, you reteach that piece of knowledge and explain how they could develop their answers to include it.

As with the conflation of feedback and marking, within this process lies the risk of a damaging misinterpretation. In this case, it is that we feel the need to constantly and artificially prove the existence of the loop. Here, we potentially find history teachers producing extensive written feedback, which students produce limited responses to, leading to the teacher producing even more extensive written feedback in an attempt to elicit a better response from the student. This can continue ad infinitum until someone collapses. Sometimes it is referred to as 360 marking or something similar. Using feedback in this way is unwieldy and a poor use of teachers' time. It also creates a learnt helplessness in our students as they know that a poorly thought-through response from them will be fixed by the teacher's comments. Educationalist Dylan Wiliam succinctly frames the thought we should always keep at the front of our minds: "The first fundamental principle of effective classroom feedback is that feedback should be more work for the recipient than the donor."[5] It is learning that is our ultimate goal, not hard proof that our chosen form of feedback has produced tangible results. Therefore, all feedback strategies for history should be rooted in manageable processes that are reciprocal and promote hard thinking in our students about how they can improve.

1. Assessment and Feedback

The starting point for our approach to feedback should be clarity on what we are trying to achieve when we assess student work, and on how this will necessarily affect the feedback we then give. Here we are going slightly off-piste as feedback is about more than just assessment; it is a process that covers all student–teacher interactions. However, as so much of our feedback is connected to assessment, it feels like a good place to start.

Any assessment must find a balance between reliability and validity. Essentially, reliability refers to the degree to which the results of the assessment are trustworthy; it is about the accuracy and consistency of the judgements made. Validity on the other hand is basically about checking that the assessment measures what it is meant to, and that we can draw useful inferences from it about what students know.[6] The problem is that as the reliability increases – by making the assessment more repeatable and replicable – often the validity decreases as the assessment becomes narrower in scope

5 Dylan Wiliam, *Embedded Formative Assessment* (Bloomington, IN: Solution Tree Press, 2011), p. 129.

6 Sarah Earle, The Challenge of Balancing Key Principles in Teacher Assessment, *Journal of Emergent Science*, 12 (2017): 41–47.

and therefore provides the assessor with less opportunity to make complex inferences. This problem also happens in reverse as assessments with high validity often allow for greater subjectivity and therefore become less reliable. There is no perfect balance between the two and so you have to accept that your assessment of students will favour one or the other.

Some examples of assessment strategies with high reliability in history would be:

- Closed question tests or quizzes.
- Verbal closed questioning of students.
- Multiple-choice questions.
- Gap-fill activities.

There is minimal chance of subjectivity in these methods of assessment and so the feedback you give would be highly reliable. In fact, the feedback may be as simple as letting students know which answers are correct and which are not, as closed questions tend to have a right and wrong answer. However, as you will notice, these approaches are only really useful for checking retention of knowledge and are therefore extremely limited if you want to check depth of understanding or assess the quality of students' writing to give precise feedback on improving it.

Our high validity assessment strategies would essentially be the extended writing tasks that drive so much of what we do. From these pieces of work, history teachers can make complex inferences about the capabilities of their students in terms of what they can do and what they know. When we mark a causation essay at the end of a unit of work on the English Reformation, we are able to judge the accuracy and depth of the knowledge students possess as well as their ability to make explicit connections between the events preceding Henry VIII's decision to break with Rome. Therefore, the inferences we can draw are deeper and more complex than those from the high reliability assessments.

It is worth noting, however, that there are also substantial limits to the wider inferences you can make from a single assessment. The causation essay on the English Reformation would not necessarily prove that students could successfully tackle a causation essay on another topic, as this success is primarily connected to the knowledge of the topic rather than simply a generic transferable skill. So, after marking those essays you will have a fairly strong idea about how well they can answer that particular question, but not necessarily about how well they will write a causation essay on the First World War.

Furthermore, we must accept that these forms of assessment have low reliability. There is a high degree of subjectivity involved in the judgements we make when assessing extended writing, one that no amount of standardisation can completely eradicate. Therefore, when we give a piece of extended writing a mark, grade or level, we cannot assume this will be replicable or repeatable in different circumstances or with a different assessor.

The implication for our use of extended writing assessments is therefore to make the majority of them formative – using them to influence future teaching – rather than summative – by assigning a grade, mark or percentage score.[7] By extension, the majority of our written feedback should be comprised of formative comments rather than summative marks, grades or levels. When we do use summative assessment, we should cover a broad span of content, as in doing so we will gain a broader idea of the knowledge and capabilities our students possess.

7 Wiliam, *Embedded Formative Assessment*, p. 37.

2. Build in Self-Reflection

As mentioned previously, one of the pitfalls of providing inordinate amounts of feedback is that it can create a learnt helplessness in students as they are conditioned to feel that the responsibility for deciding the accuracy or quality of their output lies solely with their teacher. This ties back in with the powerful effect of metacognition on learning and the importance of encouraging students to plan, monitor and evaluate their own activity. What we want our students to do is give themselves feedback before we intervene. However, be careful with this, as students can get feedback wrong. In fact, researcher Graham Nuthall found that 80% of the feedback students get is from their peers and most of it is wrong![8] By extension, the feedback they give themselves may suffer from the same inaccuracy. However, with careful scaffolding, parameters and practice, students can usefully identify problems and correct them. Some strategies for this would be:

- **Model it.** Project a worked example that you have written onto the whiteboard. Model your own editing process. What precisely would you look to improve? How would you do so?
- **Checklists.** Give students a checklist of four or five things that they will need to be confident with if they are to successfully meet the lesson objective. Use a simple colour-coded red, amber, green system for them to check

8 Nuthall, *The Hidden Lives of Learners.*

these targets against. As the lesson progresses you can stop at various points to allow opportunities for students to do some self-checking against the targets. You can then use questioning to gauge how confident they are. One for a lesson with the objective "Explain the causes of the Black Death" might look like this:

Checkpoint	Have you achieved this?
Do you know which animal carried bubonic plague and how it spread the disease to humans?	
Do you know which part of the world bubonic plague originally came from?	
Can you explain the difference between bubonic plague and pneumonic plague?	
Do you know three incorrect causes that the people of the time blamed for spreading the Black Death?	

- **Editing scaffolds.** When students are working on a piece of extended writing, display an editing scaffold for the last five to ten minutes of the task. This should prevent you having to correct too many basic errors when giving feedback. One for a Year 8 source usefulness answer might look like the following:

Read through your answer carefully and ensure you have completed the following tasks:

1. *Check your use of* capital letters *and* full stops.
2. *Check you have spelt* key terms *correctly.*
3. *Check you have made a clear point about what is* useful *about the source and write "U" in the margin alongside.*
4. *Check you have supported this point with* evidence *from the source and write "Ev" in the margin alongside.*
5. *Check you have supported this point with evidence from your own* contextual knowledge *and write "CK" in the margin alongside.*
6. *Check you have* explained *why this source is useful and write "Ex" in the margin alongside.*
7. *Check you have made a clear point about what is* limited *about the source and write "L" in the margin alongside. Repeat steps 4 and 5 to support your point about the limitations.*

- **Insist on it.** Some teachers will refuse to mark work if there is no evidence of editing. Certainly it should become an expectation, so make sure you praise students when you notice them doing it. Some students become fixated on the notion of a "perfect" book and that will mean they are reluctant to cross out and correct their work for fear of it looking messy. Make sure you encourage editing, and that students are clear you are more interested in the process of correction than on perfectly presented books.

3. Get in Early

Evidence suggests that the earlier a mistake is corrected when learning something new, the faster the information will be learnt, as you can't labour effectively under a misconception.[9] This is easy when asking closed questions to check knowledge recall or understanding; however, the principle can also be applied to extended writing. The best feedback can be that which you give while students are still in the process of purposeful practice, rather than after it has been completed, as they have the opportunity to act upon it there and then. Now, in Chapter 4 I advocated the importance of silence and of letting students get on with tasks without interruption and thus unnecessary strain on their attention. This is, therefore, another tightrope strategy, meaning you will need to make a judgement class by class and student by student about when to intervene.

Here are some strategies for giving immediate feedback in history:

- **Say it.** Verbal feedback is essential in history. First, to correct factual inaccuracies and misunderstandings, and second, to develop students' judgements. For example, during questioning, getting students to reflect on why

9 James A. Kulik and Chen-Lin C. Kulik, Timing of Feedback and Verbal Learning, *Review of Educational Research*, 58(1) (1988): 79–97.

one factor might take on greater importance than another is key to students solidifying sound judgements. Some departments will insist on teachers evidencing verbal feedback with a stamp or some sort of mark made in students' books. If this is the case then so be it, but I would question the value of this approach. The feedback is the important bit, not the evidence of it.

- **Seating plans.** Review your seating plans regularly to ensure the students who you know need the most input are within easy reach.
- **Walk with a pen in hand.** As you circulate the classroom, always keep a pen in hand to make a quick note on students' work in progress. I always use a green pen for this so that when I flick through a set of books I can recognise that I made those comments while circulating, but it is not essential to do so.
- **Write questions to spark thought.** A simple "why?" written next to an underdeveloped point in students' work can be enough to deepen thought and therefore explanation. Specific questions should be prioritised over general statements as they are more explicitly actionable – for example, "Who was the German priest whose writings inspired Protestantism?" rather than "You need to deepen your knowledge here."
- **Find the bright spots.** As discussed in Chapter 4, loudly give positive, specific feedback to an individual about the excellent piece of knowledge they have included, ensuring the whole class notices you doing so. Remember that social norms are important.
- **Spotlight an example.** Find an example with merit within the class. It could be read aloud or, even better, projected onto the whiteboard. Solicit feedback from other students about the positive aspects of the work and how it could be improved. It might take you a while to get a class to the point where you can do this successfully, but it is worth persisting.

- **Stop the bus.** Sometimes it is necessary to press the emergency stop button. If you notice that students are basically all getting something wrong, interrupt the class and reteach it.

4. Whole-Class Feedback

One antidote to what might otherwise become laborious and ineffective individual feedback is to deliver your feedback to the whole class instead. There are various benefits to this, beyond the obvious time-saving element, one of which being the degree of control it gives you over the interpretation of your feedback. Feedback succeeds or fails based on what students do with it, and if you offer thirty different pieces of individual feedback it is very difficult to control the interpretation of it. Delivering feedback to the whole class gives you greater capacity to ensure it is properly understood and therefore properly acted upon.

Former history teacher turned education researcher Harry Fletcher-Wood has written fairly extensively about whole-class feedback and proposes the following system, which he refers to as guided improvement without individual feedback:[10]

- Reteach – using fresh examples.
- Revisit goals – clarify goals with models and checklists.
- Revise the process – model the process either live or with worked examples.
- Redraft, practise and check – allow students to stay in the struggle through further practice.

10 Harry Fletcher-Wood, Guiding Student Improvement without Individual Feedback, *Improving Teaching* [blog] (18 June 2017). Available at: https://improvingteaching.co.uk/2017/06/18/guiding-student-improvement-without-individual-feedback/.

This provides a useful framework for how to approach whole-class feedback. Some further practical examples include:

- **Pick out themes when exam marking.** The biggest piece of summative marking that many teachers do is of mock exams. Giving individual targets for these is a task of near Sisyphean proportions and can feel similarly pointless given that students only want to know their grades. Therefore, when marking your mocks, score each answer but note down common misconceptions about each question, rather than providing individual feedback. Your feedback lesson can then be reteaching to address these misconceptions with the whole class.
- **Pick apart a worked example.** Rather than giving individual targets – don't worry, I do have advice for that later – following an extended writing exercise, chose one strong example and ask students to each stick a copy in the centre of a double page in their book. On the left, ask them to note down what is strong about the answer, and on the right, areas for improvement. You will need to model a few examples to get things moving.
- **Flick through a set.** Whether you mark it or not, reading your students' work is essential. Skim through a set of books and, at the start of the next lesson, clarify the purpose of the task and then outline the general areas of strength and the common barriers that prevented the desired outcomes being universally realised. This will also inform your reteaching.
- **Remodel it.** Live model your own answer to a question, explaining as you go the places where students often came up short in their work and how you would overcome this.
- **Start again.** Sometimes you will get through a few books and realise either that you just didn't teach it well enough or that they just didn't get it. Rather than wading through a whole soul-destroying set, stop, and put the time you

would have spent marking into planning a really excellent lesson to reteach the topic.

5. Create a Feedback Shorthand

This is a strategy that works best when you create your own version as it needs to be tailored to fit your context. The idea is that you create a sort of feedback shorthand through the use of symbols, abbreviations or codes. You teach the students the key to your code, and then use it when you give written feedback. It may seem a minor intervention but over the course of a year the time saved will be significant. An additional benefit is that it forces the students to think deeper, as they are required to remember the meaning of each part of your system. The EEF are, at the time of writing, running a large-scale study of an intervention called FLASH Marking, run on similar principles, in which English teachers give purely formative feedback using codes.[11] Once published, this will provide a useful evaluation of this type of intervention, which will also be of interest to history teachers.

Here are three examples of how this strategy could be used:

- **Positive comment marking.** This will help you avoid making the "well done" type of comment that is likely to have little impact. Students can write the full meaning of the code alongside or, especially as they become more familiar with it, you can dispense with this element. In the following example – for an explanation and judgement essay – the number of stars denotes relative quality and the symbol represents the specific element you wish to praise. So if you wanted to praise an excellent, balanced argument you would write ***III.

---

11 See https://educationendowmentfoundation.org.uk/projects-and-evaluation/projects/flash-marking/.

** Good*

*** Very good*

**** Excellent*

I – explanation on one side of the argument

II – use of contextual knowledge

III – balanced argument

IV – conclusion

V – relevance to the question

VI – explanation on both sides of the argument

- **T is for target.** If you wish to give individual targets, inevitably there will be several students in the class with shared goals. Rather than writing targets out in full multiple times on students' work, write each one you encounter on a PowerPoint slide, or a piece of paper, and give it a numbered code; T1, T2, and so on. You simply write the code on the students' work and each student writes out their given targets when the assessed work is handed back. The further benefit is that the next time you use that assessment, you may only need to add a few new targets to your list, based on that class' outcomes. Remember the guidance from the EEF report here and aim to make the targets as specific and actionable as possible.[12] An example for a "how far do you agree" judgement question on the Battle of Hastings could look like this:

T1: Add another reason from your knowledge that is not provided by the question – i.e. not about troops or tactics.

T2: Link your explanation back to the question by using the key words you have identified.

---

12 Elliott et al., *A Marked Improvement?*, p. 5.

T3: Make sure you have three clear, separate paragraphs each with a distinct idea.

T4: Ensure that your explanation clearly connects to your evidence by using connective phrases, such as "this meant that".

T5: Use specific terms from your knowledge organiser – for example, feigned retreat, shield wall, fyrd, and so on.

T6: Ensure your conclusion has a "clinching argument" and does not just repeat the explanation from your earlier paragraphs.

The health warning with this system is that the targets will need further explanation from you. You will need to specifically teach how these targets can be actioned. If the students did not do these things the first time round, a target telling them to will not miraculously arm them with the ability to do so – see the next strategy for ideas on how to do this. In essence, telling a student that they have not explained well will not show them how to do it effectively – you will need to do that. This is where feedback finds its limitations and reveals how flimsy a tool it is for transmitting a new concept in and of itself.

- **Use the margin.** As you attempt to get students to write structurally sound paragraphs, develop a shorthand to use in the margins to help students identify where and how effectively they are recreating the structure you have explained and modelled. For example, when marking an importance question you might use:

  P: point

  CK: contextual knowledge

  BEx: brief explanation

  DEx: developed explanation

Students will learn to look out for your margin shorthand and it will help them to recognise the make-up of their paragraphs.

6. Expect a Response

If students are unlikely to benefit from marking unless time is set aside for them to consider and act upon it, then we must insist on a response and give them time to provide one. In recent years many schools have attempted to facilitate this through the use of dedicated improvement and reflection time (DIRT), a strategy which originally appeared in Jackie Beere's *The Perfect Ofsted Lesson.*[13] The concept is simple: ring-fence time for students to respond to your marking.

I always start my DIRT lessons with something relatively simple that all students can do collectively. Often I will start

13 Jackie Beere, *The Perfect Ofsted Lesson*, rev edn (Carmarthen: Independent Thinking Press, 2012), p. 29.

by going through a worked example from the class to model the strategies, as I have mentioned previously. I may then ask them to tick all the facts or specific pieces of knowledge that the model answer contains. Next, the students will use their knowledge organisers and identify any key words they have used in their own answers.

From here the DIRT lesson could go in various directions:

- We collectively pick apart the specific strengths and weaknesses of the model answer. As mentioned in Strategy 4, students stick a copy in the middle of a double page in their books and put positive comments on the left and development points on the right, initially modelled by the teacher on the whiteboard. Once the process is completed, students redraft a section of their answer.
- Students respond to their individual targets by redrafting their whole answer or a section of it. Beware, as this will get messy and you will need to be on your toes to unstick and help students throughout. In order to make this run more smoothly you could apply the targets to a worked example first, demonstrating how they could be interpreted and actioned to improve the answer. The more targets in the room the harder this will become, so try to direct this towards fewer targets or establish specific tasks for groups of students whose targets are largely the same. For example, one task for those whose answers lacked structure, one for those who lacked knowledge and one for those who lacked developed explanation.
- Rather than rewriting whole answers, students use a different coloured pen and edit their existing work. I like the use of asterisks to develop sentences, as this works particularly well when attempting to further explanation.
- Students do not redraft their answers but instead give extended answers to the questions you have posed next to their writing. This can be an alternative to writing targets and benefits from the fact that as long as the questions are clear and understandable there is less risk

of misinterpretation. Just make sure students have access to the answers even if they missed the lesson when the knowledge was first taught.

- Identify the key word, or words, from the question. Ask students to find opportunities within their answers to replace existing vocabulary with these words. Again, modelling this first with a worked example will be important.
- Write an answer to a new, but similar, question.

Classroom culture will be important to all of these tasks, which sees us return to the principle of challenge. Students need to see the value of DIRT and be prepared to struggle through it. If they don't, and are not, you will find these lessons frustrating and start to avoid them. Always consider the purpose of the DIRT tasks being completed and ask yourself whether they will help students to do a similar piece of work better next time.

Reflective Questions

- Have you considered all the mediums for feedback that are open to you?
- Are you relying too heavily on written feedback?
- Have your students developed learnt helplessness?
- Are students using the feedback you give them?
- Are students given sufficient time and guidance to interpret and use your feedback?

Chapter 6
Questioning

Mr Grove and the dominant voice

It is Tuesday morning and Claire's voice is once again ringing around the classroom, and the ears of her Year 11 classmates. Her passion for history is clear and, although Claire's teacher realises he tends to allow her to dominate the discussion, her answers are always accurate and insightful so Mr Grove finds it hard to stop himself favouring her when the hands shoot up. More recently, hands have largely been dispensed with and almost as soon as Mr Grove's question has left his lips, Claire is starting her answer. As her latest response reaches its conclusion Mr Grove asks the class whether anyone else would like to add to what Claire has said. They stare blankly back. Mr Grove decides to take the plunge and asks Robert to give his views. Robert replies with, "Sorry, sir, what was the question?"

Questioning takes its place as the final of the six principles not due to any relative reduction in importance, but due to its ubiquity. Similar to challenge, questioning will pervade everything we do as history teachers. The remaining four principles tend to take on a position within a learning cycle.

We will often explain first, model prior to practice, insist on practice when students are ready to try something out themselves, and give feedback once we've established what students do or do not know or can or cannot do. However, we use questioning throughout our teaching; sometimes to punctuate a process, sometimes as a stand-alone strategy that may continue for twenty minutes.

Before we examine its importance, it is worth acknowledging that, aside from its obvious value, questioning represents – for me at least – the most enjoyable and fulfilling part of teaching history. The ability of a question to generate responses from our students that challenge, frustrate, amuse, surprise or, at their very best, fill us with pride never diminishes, no matter how long we have taught for. The reason why I never tire of teaching a subject like Nazi Germany, no matter how many hundreds of students I have delivered the same content to, is because the reaction of each group is different. Their responses will always carry subtle variations and, as you coax them into thinking increasingly deeply about the content through skilful questioning, you get to see and feel their understanding develop.

If explanation is the master skill of a history teacher then questioning is its closest companion. While we use questioning in a multitude of ways, it is our most powerful tool for deepening learning as it provides a mechanism for elaboration. Since the time of Socrates over two millennia ago, probing questioning has been used to challenge students to think deeper, and by teachers to remind themselves never to accept incomplete answers. The concept of constantly asking students to elaborate until their understanding is clearly demonstrated is at the core of all good history teaching, as it elevates the topics we teach beyond the abstract by bringing the past to life in the minds of our students.

The most common elaboration question in history is to ask why. Whether it is why something happened (causation), why something was important (significance) or why a source is trustworthy (reliability), asking for reasons and linking cause to outcome is essential. Questioning, alongside our own explanation, provides the best opportunity to guide students through these judgements. The judgements we support students to make are often murky and without a definitive answer, which is why skilful questioning is so important to the successful delivery of our discipline. To draw a comparison with physics, the question, "Why does nuclear fusion happen in stars?" has a definitive answer; however, the question, "Why was the slave trade abolished in Britain?" does not. Therefore, our questioning is about so much more than comprehension – although this remains a vital function of it. It is our chance to stimulate the debate that forms such a fundamental part of our subject.

Having said this, what I am certainly not suggesting is that certain types of question are inherently better than others and that we should invoke strict questioning hierarchies in history. When considering the nature of the questions we ask, we must be again be cautious not to stray from the disciplinary to the generic. Our so-called critical thinking questions are essential but they cannot be neatly pigeonholed. Elaboration questions will often deepen learning by probing the fine detail of the particular topic we are teaching. Therefore, to try to codify the specific skills-based goals these questions aim to achieve is an artificial and unnecessary additional layer. When I trained to teach, Bloom's taxonomy was often used as a framework with which to plan and structure questions. Named after its originator, the American educational psychologist Benjamin Bloom, the taxonomy is a hierarchical model used to classify learning. The problems with using Bloom's taxonomy for history teaching have been discussed by Michael Fordham and Christine Counsell, with the central criticism being that it confuses and constricts, and therefore offers no tangible benefit for students.[1] Essentially it is square peg in round hole

1 Michael Fordham, My Beef with Bloom's, *Clio Et Cetera* [blog] (28 September 2014). Available at: https://clioetcetera.com/2014/09/28/my-beef-with-blooms/.

stuff. A hierarchy in which *understand* is step two, and the somewhat nebulous term *evaluate* – or latterly *create* – is at the summit, is simply incompatible with our discipline. In order to comprehend or understand history we must simultaneously evaluate it, and so the hierarchy collapses.

To exemplify the problem, a series of questions I might have planned to teach the League of Nations during my teacher training – when I was required to use Bloom's taxonomy, specifically the revised 2000 version – might have looked like this:[2]

Remember	*Which European country did the League impose economic sanctions on in 1935?*
Understand	*Why did the League use economic sanctions?*
Apply	*How could sanctions have solved the dispute?*
Analyse	*Does this connect to any other decisions the League made?*
Evaluate	*Was the League right to act in this way?*
Create	*What might have been a more successful approach for the League to have taken?*

For me, the most useful questions here are remember, understand, analyse and evaluate. The other two, although legitimate questions to ask, are rather speculative and in my experience are unlikely to generate many useful responses; instead they could potentially confuse students. The main issue, though, is not with the questions themselves but with assuming that they can be neatly ordered into a hierarchy of difficulty. The understand question is huge, and to answer it properly requires deep knowledge of the flawed nature of

2 Lorin W. Anderson and David R. Krathwohl (eds), *A Taxonomy for Learning, Teaching, and Assessing: A Revision of Bloom's Taxonomy of Educational Objectives* (New York: Pearson, 2000).

the League, the growth of nationalism in the 1930s and the roots of appeasement, along with a wealth of other contextual factors. If I had used these questions in a lesson, it is likely that either the understand question would have led to so many follow-up questions we would be stuck there, or – and this would be worse – I would have reluctantly accepted a simplistic answer and then dutifully ploughed through the remaining questions. Rather than working to incrementally deepen students' understanding, this bout of questioning would have skimmed across the surface of the topic without securing the sort of deep knowledge from which accurate historical judgements can be made.

Therefore, a better bank of questions – not necessarily to be asked in this sequence – to interrogate the subject would look like this:

Which European country did the League impose economic sanctions on in 1935?

What are economic sanctions?

Why did the League use economic sanctions?

Why did the League fail to use military force?

How does the lack of military force link to the in-built flaws of the League?

What else was going on in Europe in 1935?

Did any contemporary events affect the League's decision in 1935?

Why did Britain and France fail to back the League against Italy?

Why were Britain and France concerned about Italy's reaction to the use of greater force?

Did economic sanctions prove the League had failed?

To fit these questions into a hierarchy would not improve their effectiveness, and I suspect if you asked a group of history teachers to rank these questions according to Bloom's taxonomy they would all have different opinions. Therefore, rather than thinking in terms of frameworks and hierarchies, it is better to think in terms of purpose. What do we want our questioning to achieve? In answer to this, there are essentially five main reasons for asking our students questions:

1. To test understanding of a new concept.
2. To deepen and develop understanding.
3. To ensure that they take a share in the cognitive work of the classroom.
4. To help you form and sustain your classroom culture.
5. To create curiosity.[3]

Of these, the first two are our most common purposes. Often we might ask slightly narrower, closed questions to test understanding, and more complex, open questions when we wish to deepen and develop it. As part of an excellent review of the evidence around classroom questioning, education researcher Kathleen Cotton defines these two types of question as lower cognitive questions and higher cognitive questions.[4] Lower cognitive questions are essentially about knowledge recall whereas higher cognitive questions

3 As outlined by Allison and Tharby, *Making Every Lesson Count*, pp. 203–204.

4 Kathleen Cotton, Close-Up #5 – Classroom Questioning, School Improvement Research Series 3 (2001). Available at: http://educationnorthwest.org/sites/default/files/ClassroomQuestioning.pdf.

require students to manipulate their knowledge in order to support a logically reasoned response. This simplified differentiation also helps give clarity to our aims when questioning.

From the previous bank of examples about the League of Nations, a lower cognitive question would be:

Which European country did the League impose economic sanctions on in 1935?

While a higher cognitive question would be:

Why did the League use economic sanctions?

Both are essential and should not be seen as necessarily better or worse than the other; rather, they perform different functions. Cotton's review reveals that lower cognitive questions are more useful for improving recall or committing new knowledge to memory. Of course, the question needs to elicit the correct response in order to avoid misconceptions being embedded.

The purpose of higher cognitive questions in history is to deepen understanding. As mentioned previously, this forms an essential phase of our teaching as we develop students' knowledge of the past beyond the basic facts, allowing them to enter into discussion and, ultimately, form judgements.

Cotton's review also found that about 60% of questions asked by teachers in the study were lower cognitive, about 20% higher cognitive and about 20% procedural.[5] Ideally this ratio would alter to see a greater proportion of higher cognitive questions asked. However, this would be contingent on the class and the context. For example, if you were recapping a large section of factual content from the

---

5 Cotton, Close-Up #5 – Classroom Questioning.

curriculum you may choose to ask a greater number of lower cognitive questions.

However, for all its importance, questioning can be one of the most frustrating aspects of teaching history when it goes wrong. Therefore, the strategies that follow are designed to help our questioning be more successful, more consistently.

1. Questioning for All

The biggest problem with Mr Grove's questioning is that it lets every other student in his class off the hook. Rosenshine tells us to, "Ask a large number of questions and check for understanding," and to, "Check the responses of all students."[6] Therefore, if we let our Claires dominate the discussion then we are doing the rest of our students a disservice. It can be an easy trap to fall into: you want the lesson to flow and you want the answers you get to support that by being accurate and insightful. As a result, you can find yourself always selecting the same handful of students to answer your questions because you know you can rely on them. The problem here is that the rest of the class will disengage and stop thinking about the topic you are

6 Rosenshine, Principles of Instruction, p. 19.

teaching. This leads to the Robert effect; when you do eventually select another student to answer they are so out of the loop they cannot remember the question. You then either move on from that student or spend a substantial amount of time scaffolding an answer for them – although sometimes this is necessary and we will return to this in Strategy 2. A second, but no less damaging, problem is that you will be unable to make accurate inferences about the learning of any student other than the one dominating the responses.

The solution is to use questioning techniques that force all students to think about their answer even if they do not provide it to the class. It also helps to vary your approach so that students do not have the option to disengage. Essentially there are three approaches to questioning in this way:

1. Hands-up

This is the traditional approach and I would argue that it still has its place in the history classroom. For one thing, it can be a useful way of gauging the class' confidence with a particular piece of knowledge by scanning how many hands go up. Although, as a caveat, if your students are used to never being asked this will need to be built up as they initially might not put their hands up whether they know the answer or not. Also there may be times when you ask a really tricky question or one that creates a bit of vulnerability in the student who answers, for example:

Do you believe every SS guard who worked in the death camps during the Second World War retains responsibility for the Holocaust?

The student who answers this may say something that others vehemently disagree with. Therefore, randomly choosing students to answer these types of questions, while not necessarily wrong, can backfire as it may create a deal of anxiety in the class. By employing hands-up questioning you get to see who feels confident or comfortable answering. Now, you might just get your usual suspects at first, but students can surprise you, and you will often find that eventually you will get less obvious candidates wishing to answer.

2. Random

This is genuinely random questioning. You can achieve this through an online name generator in which you input your students' names and it spits one out, or you could use lolly sticks with students' names on, or something similar. Or, simply pick one out at random. The benefit to this approach is that all students must be prepared to answer and therefore need to think about a response.

While random questioning certainly achieves the purpose of sharing the cognitive work around the class, I confess this is not my favourite approach as I find that it's a bit clunky and that it interrupts the natural flow of questioning. However, if you do use it I would suggest doing so for lower cognitive questions rather than those higher cognitive questions that you might want to target towards specific students.

3. Directed

This is when you simply choose who answers. Doug Lemov refers to this as "cold calling" and it is now a commonplace approach in classrooms.[7] This should ideally be your stock approach, as it allows you to form and sustain a culture in which all students expect to be asked a question at some point during the lesson. In doing so, you increase the

7 Doug Lemov, *Teach Like a Champion: 49 Techniques That Put Students on the Path to College* [Kindle edn] (San Francisco, CA: Jossey-Bass, 2010), loc. 2528.

thinking in the room, and achieve that vital history goal of forcing students to consider the wider implications of what they have just learnt.

The directed approach also allows you to tailor your questions to your students. You will know who in your class needs to be pushed into engaging with questions more regularly, who you want to test on that precise bit of knowledge or perhaps which lower ability student loves that particular topic and would benefit from an opportunity to showcase that confidence. A subtle tweak to directed questioning, suggested by Lemov, helps to keep the collective thinking on task: leave out the name of the student until after the question.[8]

Rather than:

James, why did the British government start transporting convicts to Australia?

Instead:

Why did the British government start transporting convicts to Australia, (pause) … *James?*

Without this tweak, as soon as the rest of the class hears James' name they know they are off the hook and so do not have to think about the question or answer.

There is one final caveat to including all students in questioning, which is that there may be some who just don't need to be pushed to answer questions in front of the class. In almost every class I teach there tends to be one or two fairly introverted characters who I just don't really question verbally. This is because the work they produce is of high quality and they are so averse to answering questions in front of their peers that to force them into it feels

8 Lemov, *Teach Like a Champion*, loc. 2703–2728.

counterproductive. From their work I know that they are doing the thinking, so I just leave them to it.

2. Wait (and Then Wait Some More)

This is one of those strategies that may not come naturally. Research shows that the average wait time between a teacher asking a question and accepting a student's answer is about one second. However, to get the greatest positive benefit, for lower cognitive questions this should increase to three seconds and for higher cognitive questions wait time should be even longer than that, with no particular upper limit.[9] Consequently, we should aim to add a significant pause for thought after posing a question.

The silence that this creates can be unnerving, particularly if students are not used to it. It is possible to fill that gap yourself, while encouraging thinking, as shown in this example:

Did the British Empire provide any benefits to India? (Pause.)

As you think about that, consider the different aspects of British rule that we have learnt about. (Pause.)

I'll be choosing someone to answer in the next five seconds. (Pause.)

Okay (pause), *Bethan, what do you think?*

Equally, you could allow some think, pair, share time here and give students thirty seconds in which to discuss the answer with the person sitting next to them before feeding back to the class. In any case, we should aim to leave a longer gap after each question. Part of your ability to do this will

9 Cotton, Close-Up #5 – Classroom Questioning.

be based on having clear questioning expectations and not allowing students to call out.

3. Serve and Return

To return to the idea of elaboration, the reward for successfully answering a question correctly should usually be a harder question. This will allow you to deepen not just the understanding of the student being questioned but also that of the students listening. Here is an example of how this might look:

Teacher: What disease spread through industrial London due to contaminated drinking water?

Student: Cholera.

Teacher: That's right. Why did it spread so quickly?

Student: Because people got their water from the same pump.

Teacher: That's true, but why was using the same pump a problem?

Student: Well, the water that came from it was coming from the Thames and had been contaminated.

Teacher: And what was the Thames contaminated with?

Student: Human and animal waste.

Teacher: Perfect, I'm going to move on to someone else now. What was the solution to this problem, (pause) ... *Leo?*

In this way you can lead students through the thinking and move directly into a class discussion on the subject. Although the initial follow-up questions should be harder, the difficulty need not continually increase, and you can switch up and down as you go.

4. What to Do About "I Don't Know"

When we ask a student a question in class they are likely to give one of the following five responses:

1. An accurate and detailed answer.
2. An accurate but underdeveloped answer.
3. A partially accurate answer, or a bit of a tangential waffle!
4. A completely inaccurate and/or irrelevant answer.
5. An "I don't know", or a blank stare.

Without doubt, the hardest to deal with is response number 5, when a student gives either a shrug of ignorance or the verbal equivalent. Rather than accepting this and simply moving on with, "Okay, can anyone help Robert out here?" we should instead provide the scaffolds to help the student reach a successful answer.

Muijs and Reynolds tell us, "The effect of achievement on self-concept is stronger than the effect of self-concept on achievement."[10] Therefore, if we want our students to see themselves as successful historians and be motivated in our subject, then helping them to answer questions confidently and correctly is a good way of achieving this. We will always encounter reluctant learners in our classrooms, but if we can give them an opportunity to get something right in front of the class then their confidence and engagement with the subject is likely to build.

Some ways around the dreaded "I don't know" are:

- **Remind them of the facts.**

  Teacher: Why was Blitzkrieg so successful?

  Student: I don't know.

  Teacher: Remember that Blitzkrieg involved a fast-paced attack using tanks, Stuka dive-bombers and armoured personnel carriers.

  Student: It was successful because the enemy were quickly overwhelmed.

- **Turn it into multiple-choice.**

  Teacher: Which country attacked America at Pearl Harbor?

  Student: I don't know.

  Teacher: Was it Japan, Germany or Italy?

  Student: Japan.

- **Let them tell you why an answer is correct.**

  Teacher: Why did radar play an important part in Britain winning the Battle of Britain?

---

10 Daniel Muijs and David Reynolds, *Effective Teaching: Evidence and Practice*, 4th edn (London: Sage, 2018). p. 163.

Student: I don't know.

Teacher: Okay, well, it allowed the British to see the German planes coming, which allowed them to coordinate their defence. Why would that have been important?

Student: Because the Germans wouldn't have been able to surprise them.

- **Rephrase it.**

Teacher: Did D-Day change the course of the war?

Student: I don't know.

Teacher: Sorry, I could have phrased that better. What I meant was, would the Allies still have won the war if D-Day had failed?

Student: Yes, I think they still would have won, but it probably would have taken longer.

Remember, there might be a whole raft of reasons why a student answers with "I don't know", from general obstructiveness to panic, cognitive overload or a lack of knowledge. You will need to judge for yourself what is going on and tailor your response accordingly. Approaches I would urge against include repeating the question without modification – or perhaps with an exasperated "Come on, we only did this last lesson …" – or chastising them for not knowing. Both responses are likely to make the student more reluctant to answer questions in future.

5. Continuums

Continuums are an immensely useful tool in history. We often require our students to make judgements, and continuums can be both a mechanism for them to do so and a springboard for questioning to probe their thinking deeper. They work particularly well when unpicking a statement, but can equally be used when comparing the relative importance of several contributory factors, the effect of a particular event in terms of causation or indeed anything that involves a judgement, such as deciding the relative level of tension at a given point.

To take an example, you could frame a lesson around the statement:

"Speculation on the stock market was the main reason for the Wall Street Crash in 1929."

Your accompanying continuum, displayed on your whiteboard, would look like this:

Agree ***Disagree***

In terms of process it could be used like this:

1 Students draw the continuum into their books.

2 If they have prior knowledge on the topic you could ask them to initially place a mark on the line that represents their viewpoint. I tend to ban the exact centre as typically this is really an "I don't know" response. If they don't have prior knowledge then you would need to teach the relevant content first.

3 You can then gauge the strength of agreement and disagreement in the room by slowly running your pen

along the continuum on your whiteboard. Ask students to put their hands up when your pen reaches the point they marked on their own line, and put their hands down again when you move past it. This will give you a Mexican wave effect and will allow you to stop and question for justification. You can also add to this with a sort of heart monitor effect by drawing spikes when you get a mass of students in one place on the continuum.

4. As the lesson progresses you can repeat this process. If students have changed their position, you can adapt your questions to ask why and use a different coloured pen to show how opinions have changed.

5. To refine this further you could split the continuum into three sections – strongly agree, partly agree and strongly disagree – as the three basic positions to take with the statement. This can then lead to modelling a conclusion to the argument.

You can also ask students to identify their position on the continuum with sticky notes, as I have done in the past. Over time though, I've found the board pen method means less time is lost to admin, as it is more conducive to regular use and requires no prior planning when you decide to do a continuum activity off the cuff.

6. Hinge Questions

Hinge questions are a way of checking whether students have properly understood something before moving on to the next chunk of learning. They can be a useful way to avoid injecting undue pace into our teaching and to resist the urge to plough through the content without checking whether students have mastered it. Essentially they take the form of multiple-choice questions, the correct answer to which can only be achieved through genuine comprehension of the material and not just guesswork. Thereby they inform the teacher as to whether they can move on, based on whether the students have understood the concept or not.

Beware, as they are tricky to implement in history and also, in line with the lessons about learning over performance from Chapter 1, we must be careful not to confuse confidence within the confines of a lesson with long-term learning. Harry Fletcher-Wood has written extensively about how hinge questions can be incorporated into history teaching and the difficulties he has found with this.[11] Among the reasons for this difficulty are the degree of judgement in history and the fact that we encounter ideas that are true across multiple time periods, both of which mean absolutes are harder to find in our subject than in science or maths. Fletcher-Wood has shared examples of hinge questions he created to test understanding of the key features of societies his students had studied.[12] I followed this approach to create a set to use at the end of a unit on the Cold War at Key Stage 3.

Students select what they think are the correct options from this list:

1 The USSR was communist.
2 The USA and the USSR fought directly against each other in armed conflict.
3 Nuclear weapons were developed by both sides.
4 Both sides competed over developments in space exploration.
5 Several smaller wars were fought because of the Cold War.
6 The Cuban missile crisis was a turning point in the Cold War.
7 The Berlin Wall was built.
8 One of the main ideas in capitalism is that all people should be equal.
9 Communism disappeared after the Cold War.
10 Roosevelt was an important Cold War leader.

This second list reveals the inaccurate responses:

1 The USSR was communist.

11 Harry Fletcher-Wood, Hinge Questions in History, *Improving Teaching* [blog] (17 August 2013). Available at: https://improvingteaching.co.uk/2013/08/17/hinge-questions-in-history/.

12 Harry Fletcher-Wood, 28 Hinge Questions to Use, Adapt and Refine, *Improving Teaching* [blog] (17 August 2013). Available at: https://improvingteaching.co.uk/2013/08/17/28-hinge-questions/.

2 ~~The USA and the USSR fought directly against each other in armed conflict.~~

3 Nuclear weapons were developed by both sides.

4 Both sides competed over developments in space exploration.

5 Several smaller wars were fought because of the Cold War.

6 The Cuban missile crisis was a turning point in the Cold War.

7 The Berlin Wall was built.

8 ~~One of the main ideas in capitalism is that all people should be equal.~~

9 ~~Communism disappeared after the Cold War.~~

10 ~~Roosevelt was an important Cold War leader.~~

Students' responses can be shared using a show of hands, mini-whiteboards or sticky notes, which would then reveal the level of understanding in the class. This would in turn inform the direction the teaching needs to take next, potentially including the reteaching of certain elements that have evidently caused confusion.

7. Questioning Pitfalls

Finally, here are some of the common mistakes made with questioning in history, learnt the hard way from my own bitter experience:

- **Playing guess what's in my head.** You have decided upon the answer you want to the higher cognitive question you've just posed and when you get a response that doesn't quite match it throws you and you end up trying to coax students to arrive at your answer. Better to dispense with the questioning and just tell them in this case.

- **Doing too much of the work yourself.** Sometimes questions can become little more than punctuation for your own explanation. You give a complex justification and then the student is expected to add a mere word on to the end, which is usually so obvious it requires very little thinking. For example:

Teacher: Neville Chamberlain was wrong to pursue appeasement because it allowed Hitler to gain strength and confidence which meant that when war finally came he could not easily be …, what?

Student: stopped.

Effective questioning should share the cognitive work, so make sure yours elicits thinking and does not just mirror your own.

- **Getting students to guess.** If a student genuinely doesn't know what happened at Dunkirk in 1940 then no amount of questioning will help, and guessing will just lead to random answers with little value. Better to just reteach.

Reflective Questions

- Do you have a clear vision of how you want questioning to run in your classroom?
- How will you deal with "I don't know" responses?
- What is the split between lower cognitive questions and higher cognitive questions in your classroom?
- Do you insist on students elaborating on their initial answers?
- Do you question the majority of the students in your classes each lesson?

Final Thoughts

The intention of this book has been to provide history teachers with underpinning theory, solid principles and, above all else, usable strategies to take away and apply in their classrooms. I firmly believe that, put to use, these ideas will lead to better teaching and more successful learning in history. By sharing these strategies I hope to have sparked some thinking that will ultimately lead to more effective history lessons. Whether this happens will be down to each teacher's personal interpretation; the person best placed to decide which strategies to adopt, which to adapt and which to ignore is you. You know best in your own classroom, and while this book promotes a certain approach to teaching history, it will be weaving elements into your own practice, rather than seeking to replicate it wholesale, that will be most effective.

It is also true to say that any book represents a snapshot in time. There are likely to be elements here that – with the passage of time, greater thought and discussion, and emerging evidence – will eventually need revision or potentially renovation. You can form part of this discussion by sharing the principles widely and adding your own critique as you apply them in context. Indeed, I'd encourage you to do so.

What this book does not claim to be is a blueprint for the perfect history lesson. I do not believe such a thing exists, and would place myself closer to pragmatist than idealist on a continuum of these principles. I have been teaching history for more than a decade and while some of the thousands of lessons I've delivered have gone as well as I could possibly have hoped, just as many have left me feeling like an imposter. Part of accepting this reality is to realise that there will be the occasional student for whom no amount of evidence-informed teaching makes the difference and we have to reluctantly admit defeat. However, part of our moral purpose is do everything in our power to resist this, and work to develop our toolbox of strategies to solve the trickiest of classroom puzzles.

To develop your practice, be judicious in your selection of strategies from this book. For some classes you will be able to select with impunity and find that almost anything will work to enhance those lessons. For others you will need to narrow your focus and simply pick three or four key approaches to find success. These decisions can only be guided by context, driven by you and your colleagues.

Some strategies can be used straight away in your next lesson while others require a more gradual cultural shift in the classroom to be truly effective. I would suggest an approach based on slow adaptation rather than immediate and radical change. Try a strategy with a class, refine it, widen it to your other classes, if applicable, and then repeat. Trying too much too quickly will muddle your thinking and confuse both you and your students.

There will be much this book has missed and every history teacher who reads it will be able to add something to enhance it. It is through our countless interactions with students that we learn how to get the best from them and from our subject. The more we share our collective wisdom, the stronger we all become.

Teach with passion but reflect with precision. By becoming more informed we improve our decision-making on how to teach, what to teach and, by extension, our ability to make every history lesson count.

Bibliography

Allison, Shaun (2014). Effective Use of Video in the Classroom, *Class Teaching* [blog] (23 January). Available at: https://classteaching.wordpress.com/2014/01/23/effective-use-of-video-in-the-classroom/.

Allison, Shaun and Andy Tharby (2015). *Making Every Lesson Count: Six Principles to Support Great Teaching and Learning* (Carmarthen: Crown House Publishing).

Anderson, Lorin W. and David R. Krathwohl (eds) (2000). *A Taxonomy for Learning, Teaching, and Assessing: A Revision of Bloom's Taxonomy of Educational Objectives* (New York: Pearson).

Beck, Isabel L., Margaret G. McKeown and Linda Kucan (2013). *Bringing Words to Life: Robust Vocabulary Instruction*, 2nd edn (New York: Guilford Press).

Beere, Jackie (2012). *The Perfect Ofsted Lesson*, rev edn (Carmarthen: Independent Thinking Press).

Carroll, Jim (2018). Duplo to Watercolours: How the Substantive Might Shape the Disciplinary in Students' Historical Causal Arguments, *J Carroll History* [blog] (2 March). Available at: https://jcarrollhistory.com/2018/03/02/duplo-to-watercolours-how-the-substantive-might-shape-the-disciplinary-in-students-causal-arguments/.

Clark, Ruth C., Frank Nguyen and John Sweller (2006). *Efficiency in Learning: Evidence-Based Guidelines to Manage Cognitive Load* (San Francisco, CA: Pfeiffer).

Coe, Robert (2016). What Makes Great Teaching?, speech at SSAT and The Prince's Teaching Institute Conference, 6 July. Available at: https://webcontent.ssatuk.co.uk/wp-content/uploads/2016/07/08132401/What-makes-great-teaching-Rob-Coe-1.pdf.

Coe, Robert, Cesare Aloisi, Steve Higgins and Lee Elliot Major (2014). *What Makes Great Teaching? Review of the Underpinning Research* (London: Sutton Trust). Available at: https://www.suttontrust.com/wp-content/uploads/2014/10/What-Makes-Great-Teaching-REPORT.pdf.

Collingwood, R. G. (1994 [1946]). *The Idea of History*, rev edn (Oxford: Oxford University Press).

Cotton, Kathleen (2001). Close-Up #5 – Classroom Questioning, School Improvement Research Series 3. Available at: http://educationnorthwest.org/sites/default/files/ClassroomQuestioning.pdf.

Dunlosky, John (2013). Strengthening the Student Toolbox: Study Strategies to Boost Learning, *American Educator*, 37(3): 12–21. Available at: https://www.aft.org/sites/default/files/periodicals/dunlosky.pdf.

Earle, Sarah (2017). The Challenge of Balancing Key Principles in Teacher Assessment, *Journal of Emergent Science*, 12: 41–47.

Ebbinghaus, Hermann (1913 [1885]). *Memory: A Contribution to Experimental Psychology*, Henry A. Ruger and Clara E. Bussenius (tr.). Available at: http://nwkpsych.rutgers.edu/~jose/courses/578_mem_learn/2012/readings/Ebbinghaus_1885.pdf.

Elliott, Victoria, Jo-Anne Baird, Therese N. Hopfenbeck, Jenni Ingram, Ian Thompson, Natalie Usher, Mae Zantout, James Richardson and Robbie Coleman (2016). *A Marked Improvement? A Review of the Evidence on Written Marking* (London: Education Endowment Foundation). Available at: https://educationendowmentfoundation.org.uk/public/files/Publications/EEF_Marking_Review_April_2016.pdf.

Fletcher-Wood, Harry (2013). 28 Hinge Questions to Use, Adapt and Refine, *Improving Teaching* [blog] (17 August). Available at: https://improvingteaching.co.uk/2013/08/17/28-hinge-questions/.

Fletcher-Wood, Harry (2013). Hinge Questions in History, *Improving Teaching* [blog] (17 August). Available at: https://improvingteaching.co.uk/2013/08/17/hinge-questions-in-history/.

Fletcher-Wood, Harry (2017). Guiding Student Improvement without Individual Feedback, *Improving Teaching* [blog] (18 June). Available at: https://improvingteaching.co.uk/2017/06/18/guiding-student-improvement-without-individual-feedback/.

Fordham, Michael (2014). Beyond Levels Part Two: Summative and Formative Assessment, *Clio Et Cetera* [blog] (18 February). Available at: https://clioetcetera.com/2014/02/18/beyond-levels-part-2-summative-and-formative-assessment/.

Fordham, Michael (2014). Levels: Where It All Went Wrong, *Clio Et Cetera* [blog] (8 February). Available at: https://clioetcetera.com/2014/02/08/levels-where-is-all-went-wrong/.

Fordham, Michael (2014). My Beef with Bloom's, *Clio Et Cetera* [blog] (28 September). Available at: https://clioetcetera.com/2014/09/28/my-beef-with-blooms/.

Fordham, Michael (2017). Substantive Concepts at KS2 & KS3, *Clio Et Cetera* [blog] (9 November). Available at: https://clioetcetera.com/2017/11/09/substantive-concepts-at-ks2-ks3/.

Gorard, Stephen, Beng Huat See and Peter Davies (2012). *The Impact of Attitudes and Aspirations on Educational Attainment and Participation* (York: The Joseph Rowntree Foundation). Available at: http://www.jrf.org.uk/sites/files/jrf/education-young-people-parents-full.pdf.

Heath, Chip and Dan Heath (2008). *Made to Stick: Why Some Ideas Take Hold and Others Come Unstuck* (London: Arrow Books).

Hill, Nicole M. and Walter Schneider (2006). Brain Changes in the Development of Expertise: Neuroanatomical and Neurophysiological

Evidence about Skill-Based Adaptations. In K. Anders Ericsson, Neil Charness, Robert R. Hoffman and Paul J. Feltovich (eds), *The Cambridge Handbook of Expertise and Expert Performance* (Cambridge: Cambridge University Press), pp. 653–682.

Hitler, Adolf (1933). Official Speech on the Enabling Act to the Reichstag, Berlin, 23 March. Available at: http://www.worldfuturefund.org/Reports2013/hitlerenablingact.htm.

Jones, Kate (2018). Retrieval Practice Challenge Grids for the Classroom, *Love to Teach* [blog] (12 January). Available at: https://lovetoteach87.com/2018/01/12/retrieval-practice-challenge-grids-for-the-classroom/.

Kirby, Joe (2015). Knowledge Organisers, *Pragmatic Education* [blog] (28 March). Available at: https://pragmaticreform.wordpress.com/2015/03/28/knowledge-organisers/.

Kluger, Avraham N. and Angelo DeNisi (1996). The Effects of Feedback Interventions on Performance: A Historical Review, a Meta-Analysis, and a Preliminary Feedback Intervention Theory, *Psychological Bulletin*, 119(2): 254–284.

Kulik, James A. and Chen-Lin C. Kulik (1988). Timing of Feedback and Verbal Learning, *Review of Educational Research*, 58(1): 79–97.

Lemov, Doug (2010). *Teach Like a Champion: 49 Techniques That Put Students on the Path to College* [Kindle edn] (San Francisco, CA: Jossey-Bass).

Lemov, Doug, Erica Woolway and Katie Yezzi (2012). *Practice Perfect: 42 Rules for Getting Better at Getting Better* (San Francisco, CA: Jossey-Bass).

Marzano, Robert J. (2004). *Building Background Knowledge for Academic Achievement: Research on What Works in Schools* (Alexandria, VA: Association for Supervision and Curriculum Development).

Muijs, Daniel and David Reynolds (2018). *Effective Teaching: Evidence and Practice*, 4th edn (London: Sage).

Newmark, Ben (2018). Am I Allowed to Sit at My Desk?, *BENNEWMARK* [blog] (16 February). Available at: https://bennewmark.wordpress.com/2018/02/16/am-i-allowed-to-sit-at-my-desk/.

Newton, E. (1990). Overconfidence in the Communication of Intent: Heard and Unheard Melodies, unpublished doctoral dissertation (Stanford, CA: Stanford University).

Nuthall, Graham (2007). *The Hidden Lives of Learners* (Wellington: New Zealand Council for Educational Research Press).

Peirce, William (2003). Metacognition: Study Strategies, Monitoring, and Motivation. Available at: http://academic.pg.cc.md.us/~wpeirce/MCCCTR/metacognition.htm.

Rawson, Katherine A., Ruthann C. Thomas and Larry L. Jacoby (2015). The Power of Examples: Illustrative Examples Enhance Conceptual

Learning of Declarative Concepts, *Educational Psychology Review*, 27(3): 483–504. Available at: https://doi.org/10.1007/s10648-014-9273-3.

Richards, Hugh (2017). Telling Stories and Teaching History, *Research Schools Network* [blog] (5 June). Available at: https://huntington.researchschool.org.uk/2017/06/05/telling-stories-and-teaching-history/.

Roediger III, Henry L., Adam L. Putnam and Megan A. Smith (2011). Ten Benefits of Testing and Their Applications to Educational Practice. In Jose P. Mestre and Brian H. Ross (eds), *The Psychology of Learning and Motivation, Volume 55: Cognition in Education* (San Diego, CA: Elsevier Academic Press), pp. 1–36. Available at: http://dx.doi.org/10.1016/B978-0-12-387691-1.00001-6.

Rosenshine, Barak (2012). Principles of Instruction: Research-Based Strategies That All Teachers Should Know, *American Educator*, 36(1): 12–19, 39. Available at: https://www.aft.org/sites/default/files/periodicals/Rosenshine.pdf.

Smith, Megan and Yana Weinstein (2016). Six Strategies for Effective Learning, *The Learning Scientists* [blog] (18 August). Available at: http://www.learningscientists.org/blog/2016/8/18-1.

Soderstrom, Nicholas C. and Robert A. Bjork (2015). Learning Versus Performance, An Integrative Review, *Perspectives on Psychological Science*, 10(2): 176–199.

Sweller, John (1994). Cognitive Load Theory, Learning Difficulty, and Instructional Design, *Learning and Instruction*, 4(4): 295–312. Available at: https://doi.org/10.1016/0959-4752(94)90003-5.

Waack, Sebastian (2016). Hattie Ranking: Backup of 138 Effects Related to Student Achievement, *Visible Learning* [blog]. Available at: https://visible-learning.org/2016/04/hattie-ranking-backup-of-138-effects/.

Wiliam, Dylan (2011). *Embedded Formative Assessment* (Bloomington, IN: Solution Tree Press).

Willingham, Daniel T. (2007). Critical Thinking, Why Is It So Hard to Teach?, *American Educator* (summer): 8–19. Available at: https://www.aft.org/sites/default/files/periodicals/Crit_Thinking.pdf.

Willingham, Daniel T. (2008–2009). What Will Improve a Student's Memory?, *American Educator* (winter) 17–25, 44. Available at: https://www.aft.org/sites/default/files/periodicals/willingham_0.pdf.

Willingham, Daniel T. (2009). *Why Don't Students Like School? A Cognitive Scientist Answers Questions About How the Mind Works and What It Means for the Classroom* (San Francisco, CA: Jossey-Bass).

Woodcock, James (2005). Does the Linguistic Release the Conceptual? Helping Year 10 to Improve Their Causal Reasoning, *Teaching History*, 119: 5–14.

Making Every Lesson Count

Six principles to support great teaching and learning

Shaun Allison and Andy Tharby

ISBN: 978-184590973-4

This award-winning title has now inspired a whole series of books. Each of the books in the series are held together by six pedagogical principles – challenge, explanation, modelling, practice, feedback and questioning – and provide simple, realistic strategies that teachers can use to develop the teaching and learning in their classrooms.

A toolkit of techniques that teachers can use every lesson to make that lesson count. No gimmicky teaching – just high-impact and focused teaching that results in great learning, every lesson, every day.

Suitable for all teachers – including trainee teachers, NQTs and experienced teachers – who want quick and easy ways to enhance their practice.

ERA Educational Book Award winner 2016. Judges' comments: "A highly practical and interesting resource with loads of information and uses to support and inspire teachers of all levels of experience. An essential staffroom book."

Making Every Science Lesson Count

Six principles to support great science teaching

Shaun Allison

ISBN: 978-178583182-9

Making Every Science Lesson Count goes in search of answers to the fundamental question that all science teachers must ask: "What can I do to help my students become the scientists of the future?"

Shaun points a sceptical finger at the fashions and myths that have pervaded science teaching over the past decade or so and presents a range of tools and techniques that will help science teachers make abstract ideas more concrete and practical demonstrations more meaningful.

Making Every English Lesson Count

Six principles to support great reading and writing

Andy Tharby

ISBN: 978-178583179-9

Brings the teaching of conceptual knowledge, vocabulary and challenging literature to the foreground and shows teachers how to develop students' reading and writing proficiency over time.

Andy taps into the transformational effect that quality English teaching can have, and talks secondary school English teachers through effective methods that will challenge students to read and think beyond the confines of their world.

Making Every Primary Lesson Count

Six principles to support great teaching and learning

Jo Payne and Mel Scott

ISBN: 978-178583181-2

Shares a host of strategies designed to cultivate a growth mindset in the primary school classroom and guide children towards independence: motivating both teachers and pupils to aim high and put in the effort required to be successful in all subject areas.

Jo and Mel also offer tips on how to implement effective routines and procedures so that students are clear about what is expected from them.

Making Every Maths Lesson Count

Six principles to support great maths teaching

Emma McCrea

ISBN: 978-178583332-8

Making Every Maths Lesson Count provides practical solutions to perennial problems and inspires a rich, challenging and evidence-based approach to secondary school maths teaching.

Emma shares gimmick-free advice that combines the time-honoured wisdom of excellent maths teachers with the most useful evidence from cognitive science – enabling educators to improve their students' conceptual understanding of maths over time.

Making Every Geography Lesson Count

Six principles to support great geography teaching

Mark Enser

ISBN: 978-178583339-7

Maps out the key elements of effective geography teaching to help teachers ensure that their students leave their lessons with an improved knowledge of the world, a better understanding of how it works and the geographical skills to support their understanding.

Mark offers an inspiring alternative to restrictive Ofsted-driven definitions of great teaching, and empowers geography teachers to deliver great lessons and celebrate high-quality practice.